FORGED IN FIRE:
From Fear to Faith

by

Jimmy Gleason

First Edition

Gleason Books

Copyright © by Jimmy Gleason 2018

All rights reserved. No part of this book may be reproduced, copied, stored, shared, translated, distributed or transmitted in any printed or electronic form, or by any means whatsoever graphic, electronic, or mechanical, including but not limited to photocopying, scanning, recording, or information storage and retrieval system without the prior written permission of the Author.

First Edition, 2018,

1 2 3 4 5 6 7 8 9 10 LSI 23 22 21 20 19 18
Set in Cambria and Garamond.

International Standard Book Number: 978-0-9994978-0-7

Jimmy Gleason, professional tennis player, coach, author and inspirational speaker resides in Laguna Beach, CA.

Contact Jimmy at :
gleasontennis@yahoo.com or coachjimmyg.com.

CONTENTS

The Phoenix — xi

Chapter 1	The Storm and the Breakdown: Sign of the Times	1
Chapter 2	Kicked Out of the Nest and Learning to Fly	5
Chapter 3	Summer Cometh and the Family	9
Chapter 4	Mama's Broken Heart	23
Chapter 5	Healing is in the Air	29
Chapter 6	The Giver	33
Chapter 7	Mommy Dearest	37
Chapter 8	Dr. Jekyl & Mr. Hyde's & Dad's Retirement Party	43
Chapter 9	Tennis My New Passion	51
Chapter 10	Floppy Shoes and the Tennis House	55
Chapter 11	The Coach: Mr. Positive	59
Chapter 12	Catching the Bus and the Wake-up Call	63
Chapter 13	True Commitment	69
Chapter 14	Funny Family Stories	75

Chapter 15	High School Years and The Journey to Indy	81
Chapter 16	Goodbye Daddy Hello Father	93
Chapter 17	Western Michigan University Tennis & the Miracle Woman	103
Chapter 18	She's Gone	111
Chapter 19	Summer in Saipan, a Summer of Healing	121
Chapter 20	CLC, Rodney King, and Amway	125
Chapter 21	California Dreaming	137
Chapter 22	Goodbye My Friend	143

ACKNOWLEDGEMENTS

I want to thank my mom and dad, who are the greatest heroes in my life for always being there for me and being the loving example of integrity that I still look up to till this very day. To my 11 brothers and sisters, who I love dearly and have always been there for me whenever I needed them. To all my great friends, teachers, pastors and mentors: Big Steve Ray, Michael Small, Pastor Joel Brooks, Pastor Ervin Armstrong, Jen Skiba, Tim Rogers, Roy Griffin, Pastor Jay Grant, the Bowen family, Garry Glaub, The Romeo family, Ginger Dahlem, Peter Nez, Glenn Parrish, Murphy Richardson, Bishop Noel Jones, Robin Tench, Dexter Yager, Tommy Gleason (for witnessing to me and then leading me to the Lord), Dr. Steve Boden, Terry Haymond, Nancy Farrand, Steve Riggs, Victor Ranches, Les Dodson, Coach Jack Vredeveldt, Bill Adams, Leonard and Joyce Irvine, Gregory Moore, Jon and Julie Knowlton, Kris and Tangi Fountain, Layla Jabboori, Gail Crittenden, Shawna Smith, Pastor Brian Parsons, Maleeka Love, Eugene Reyes, Donnie and Mary Lewis, Myron Cobbs, Charles Welch, Big Doug Wright, Kevin and Kita Moore, Cynthia Smith, Kevin Crosky, Gill Garrett, Arvelle Craig, Marco McGrinson, Brad and Kim DeHaven, Steve and Cindy Johnson, Jerry Meadows, Felicia Taylor, Lord Byron Scott, John Rushing, George and Ruth Halsey, Phil and Eunice Mitchel, Steven E. Schmitt, Kim Baldwin, Jennifer Dudley, Mandell and Tonya Frazier, Pastor Hosea Collins, Roman Collins, Eddie Felton, Brian Bates, Pastor Seth Gaiters, The Armstrong Family, Jaydeep Purandar and The Hahn Family, Jackie and Hugh Anderson, The McCarty Family, The Doster Family, Helen Burrel, Randy, Ryan & Kiley Johnson, Barbara Parfet, John Buckley, The Harrington Family, Meghna Sinha, Kent Armstrong, Aaron Talarico, Mike McMcray, Effy Shirazi, Farshid Khodaei, John Carpenter, Oscar Wegner, Lucile Bosche', Ashanti Bryant, Aaron and Justin Taylor,

Steve Taylor, Pat Fox, Jeanette Anderson, Mark Standish, Aubrey Lipsey, The Page family, Hal Jolley, and Ed Nagle. Most importantly, I thank my Lord and Savior, Jesus Christ, for choosing me to be His and walking me through my destiny as it unfolds. To friends I may have missed, thank you from the bottom of my heart for being there for me and for helping me on my journey.

BISHOP'S TESTIMONY

For God did not give us a spirit of fear, but of power, love, and a sound mind. This book shows you how to be victorious through faith and have a powerful mindset to look at trials as precious opportunities to gain experience at being an overcomer. This book was written to inspire people to never give up in life so that they can reach all their goals and dreams in life and ultimately realize their destiny

Jimmy as a child

THE PHOENIX

Death has followed me all my life. Haunting whispers commune with me late in the midnight hour. Nobody hears my cries because loneliness and fear constrict around me, leaving me feeling deadened on the inside. The tears never come out; they stay on the inside. He tries to quench my spirit and extinguish my flame, but hope always appears just in time. In fact, it never leaves me. It always resides inside. Every time, I rise... When I was young, I rode on a ship not of my choosing, bullied by fear, depression and their cousin despair. Many times I felt paralyzed in their presence. I see those I love and a distant shore. I yell for them, but they can't hear me. They don't realize how much they are in my thoughts and always in my heart. They are the reason I hope, the reason I dream. They are the reason I rise. As I got older I found a new ship and a new captain with a glint in his eyes. Many times I can't see him except I hear a gentle faint whisper and it says to me press on. I have met many who have come aboard the ship; we have traveled to distant shores and fought many battles together. I have lost many dear to me, leaving me in a heap of ashes. But like a phoenix, I rise. It feels now like my journey is just beginning, as destiny's call is just on the horizon. Hope inside me is ever faithful and love powerfully spurs me on. It is because of them, like a phoenix, I rise.

Chapter 1

The Storm and The Breakdown: A Sign Of The Times

This is my story and my hope is it truly blesses and inspires those I love including my family, friends and the world at large to live their life with vision, purpose and most of all to never quit. It was a stormy October evening in 1972 when my mother sent me up to my sister's bedroom to take a nap. I ran up to the window and raised my hands and face to the glass, peering out in awe of the ferocity of the storm. Rain poured down like an avalanche lightning coursed through the sky and thunder exploded all around me. Each time I would recoil from the window and then cautiously would come back to the window to watch the raw power of what nature had to offer. It was very dark in the room and I was always scared of the dark. But slowly, I began to tire. The only light I had was the bright light of the lightning that would light up the room like a giant firefly. I slowly crawled up to the bed and tucked myself under the covers and held tight the pillow, a natural reflex for me when I was scared. As the storm raged on, I fell into a deep sleep. Then I had the most terrifying dream a 2 ½-year-old could ever have. The storm followed me into my dream and I was caught in a vicious whirlpool with no means of escape. Completely terrified, I spiraled down into it and I couldn't breathe. My heart was racing and just when I thought I was about to perish, the dream ended. Looking back at this dream, I now realize that it was more than just a dream of a little child; it was a sign of things to come.

I am the youngest of a large family of 12 children. I remember my life and many specific memories from a very young age. I can remember counting my age from at least the age of two. My earliest memories of my mother were very fond ones. I remember mom with a big smile and great love in her eyes. She was a woman full of energy and passion. She was always doing motherly work such as laundry, cleaning the house or making homemade meals, which she did every day. Mom was always super busy... Of course, she was always making home-cooked meals because she certainly could not afford to take us out very often to eat because of our number. I remember my mom enjoyed folding laundry in front of the TV while watching her favorite soap opera. I enjoyed helping her. It was usually right after the clothes came out of the dryer, and I could feel the heat from the laundry, which felt nice to my skin. I had no idea what was going on with mom's soap operas and they bored me to tears at that age. The only show that interested me was the Price Is Right. Who wouldn't love that show?

My father was a traditional working man. He worked a 9 to 5 job as a manager at the Brown company, which was the main paper company in the city of Kalamazoo. He was a tremendous provider and loved all of us, especially our mom. To my father, mom was the queen. My dad was a two-sport college star in football and basketball at Kalamazoo College. He was very laid-back, the exact opposite of my mother. When I saw them together, I knew they were in love. It really affects the family in such a positive way when their parents love each other for real. Their love for each other was constant and sure as the rising of the sun. Even though our family had its trouble and turmoil, it was hardly ever between them. It was obvious they really loved each other.

When dad would come home from work, he would always have at least one, maybe two, Miller beers to unwind while reading the newspaper. Many times I'd sit on his lap as he read. My father never talked about his sports exploits and I only heard about it from some of my dad's old buddies he grew up with. My dad never tooted his own horn; he was a humble man. My dad was 49 years old when I was born, so he always seemed older to me because he had grey hair and had already gone bald. Later, when I got older, I saw pictures of him when he was young and I was shocked at how good-looking he was. My first thought was that he looked like a movie star.

It was a year later after my dream, during the thunderstorm, that my life changed forever. I was not much more than three years old and I was alone in our family room just playing on the carpet in the dark. I was just daydreaming innocent thoughts of a child. As I looked up at the light in the kitchen, I saw a figure come towards me from the light and into the darkness with me. I could not tell who it was at first until the figure knelt down in front of me because the light was so bright. That person was my mother. She looked into my eyes. I noticed her eyes were bloodshot and she was groaning. As I kept looking at her, she started to slowly pull her hair out like she was trying to pull out the pain. She needed someone to be there for her and I believe God chose me. I instinctively put my little arms around her and let her cry and groan. She was having a nervous breakdown. That night, my mom's pain leapt into my soul and her pain became mine. It was that night that I became her protector. Her pain bound us together forever. After that night, I was baptized by fire and on my way to becoming an old soul.

Wisdom Nuggets

1) Pain is the necessary ingredient for destiny. Remember that God is in control. There are no accidents. When God allows something traumatic, like what happened to me and my mother's nervous breakdown, He had more than me in mind. The pain burned compassion in me, which I have used to help 100's if not thousands of other people. I call it God's Big Love Plan.

2) The power of God's Grace. As I look back, I realize it was God's grace that allowed me to bend and not break with this first of many trials. In Romans 8:37, when God says, "We are more than conquerors through Christ who strengthens us." He is serious about allowing us to go through great trials to become more than Conquerors. That's why it's critical that we learn to trust God or it can be easy to think he is abusive or doesn't care. Every great leader in the bible, from Joseph to Jesus, went through great trials and heartache. It was their pathway to greatness. Don't run, but just stand.

Chapter 2

Kicked Out of the Nest and Learning To Fly

Fast forward to a couple of years later, I started kindergarten at Comstock North Elementary. Out of the protective cocoon of home, I was thrown into a sea of other kids my age, everything so unfamiliar and unsettling. The teacher was Mrs. McPhee. I liked her right away. Not long after being in school, I noticed school was hard for me and the lessons I was being taught many times were difficult for me to follow. I always felt like I was behind and didn't understand what was going on. Early on, that built an intense hunger in me to want to succeed and keep up with the smart kids. I remember always trying hard and wanting to do well. The problem was that no matter how hard I tried, I would often get bored and would daydream. If something interested me, I had no trouble focusing. Of course, the playground was my favorite place to be and I was already good at sports, so I felt good about myself out there. Whether we were playing kickball, marbles, or just playing tag, I loved being physically active.

My brothers and many of my sisters were very athletic. I got exposed to baseball before I was three years old. My brothers, I remember, used to collect baseball cards. Their favorite player was Willie Horton from the Detroit Tigers. The Tigers had won the World Series in 1968, the year before I was born, so Willie Horton was one of the big stars that year in the Detroit Tigers win. I found out that my brother, Pat, wanted to name me Willie after the famous Detroit Tiger. To my brothers, David, Stevie & Pat, baseball was everything. They would be in the backyard whipping the baseball around and I mean with some serious velocity. We used to play a game called hotbox, where you are in the middle of two bases trying to not get tagged out. Pat, my oldest brother, Stevie and David, who are just two years older than me, were all pitchers and that's what I became.

I was lucky to have them as such powerful influences and mentors.

Sports was my outlet and I thank God it came easily to me. Pat, the oldest boy was the unquestioned leader and could be a little scary and intimidating. Fortunately for me, he liked me and only my mom and him called me Jamie. Our house attracted many of the neighborhood kids and we would play all kinds of sports and games out in the street and in the yard... At the left corner of our front yard, there was a small dirt area to play marbles and kids would stop by there and play. I played marbles sometimes but usually watched my brother, David take everyone's marbles when he won the games. There were also tons of bikes, especially banana bikes the younger kids would ride all over the neighborhood. One of the most popular bikes was a stingray. I actually didn't get a bike until I was 10. It took me awhile to get used to riding a bike. I wasn't very good and felt like I was going to fall half the time.

In the 70s, video games were not around yet. Given that I was from Michigan the different seasons gave us lots of options. In the fall, it was football, winter sliding, snowball fights and road hockey. Springtime meant kite flying & baseball. Of course, every season except winter, we played games like kick the can and bloody murder. Kick the can is a game where one person is picked to find people who are hiding and tag them out. At the same time, they have to guard this can because if anyone kicked it, he or she lost the game. Bloody murder involved hiding from a chosen person who was trying to catch you. The darker it got, the more fun playing bloody murder was because you were being chased in the dark and you constantly had to be watchful of this person. Both these games were high-octane, adrenaline-pumping, and a complete blast. I have such fond memories of these games and was always included at such a young age. I liked how we would just gather friends from close by houses and just come together and make up our own fun.

Everything was done outdoors then. Even at that young age, I would go with my older brothers and their friends and we would go to a street called H Avenue. There was a path up a hill and we would walk until there was nothing but open fields coupled with some huge and slightly treacherous rocky hills. If you kept going, you would run into pine tree forests and eventually a beautiful small creek. There was so much beautiful nature to explore and no housing development at that time. We had no worries about safety back then. As long as we didn't go out alone, our parents weren't worried. It was a simple life and a great place for a kid to grow up. I remember distinctly not wanting to come inside as dawn was approaching. Most of the time, before it really got too dark, we would be called inside by our parents, but we all wanted to stay out longer. Growing up in our middle-class neighborhood was a privilege. Thinking back to those times with every member of my family and all the neighborhood friends we had, I really miss those times.

When I didn't have anyone to play with, I was fine and my favorite place to practice all the sports I played was in the backyard. Back there, we had a picnic table and my mom's garden was on the other side of the yard. There were trees at the left and right corner of our yard, with 3 fledgling pine trees, which were just planted to fill in the middle gap. What I practiced most back there was hitting a baseball as far as I could and kicking a football. Of course, it was always more fun to do it with one of my brothers, usually David. I loved the backyard because there was so much flat open space. Next door to us were our neighbors, the Vetti's and sometimes the ball would go over their wooden fence and I had to climb over and get it. They also had a nice pool at their house, which we dove in a few times over the years when they weren't home. Terry, their son, went to school with some of my older brothers, but he was more Pat and Kelly's age. At the other end of our yard was a huge open field that was undeveloped. That was where all the neighborhood kids would fly kites. At times there would be over 20 kites up in that field during the springtime.

Wisdom Nuggets

3) Embrace the cards you are dealt. Right when I got into school, I realized it was going to be a difficult ride. Feeling like I was slow in school, I knew I had to put up a fight, show commitment and bring out the competitiveness in me so I could always finish everything. This helped me all through school and I even got two degrees in

college. Later on, while I was studying for my second degree in physical education, I decided to get tested to see if I had a learning disability. It turned out I have what is classified as attention deficit disorder with hyperactivity or ADHD. This was the main reason I struggled so much.

4) Have a positive attitude. I love the adage that says, "Your attitude determines your altitude." It's so true. I may have had my struggles as a student, but my fight and never-give-up spirit made up for it. Maybe your weakness is not as glaring as mine with ADHD, but at some point in your life something earthshaking will come your way and you will have to fight or be defeated. I say to you, never ever give up and you won't be defeated. It's a must that you become flexible and learn to bend with the punches thrown at you. Once you build your attitude and that inner you, there is nothing you can't do or become.

Chapter 3

Summer Cometh and The Family

I made it through kindergarten and made many new friends. I found out where I fit in a little bit with my peers. Summer was coming and I knew what that meant—watching my brother's baseball games and the annual migration out to our summer cottage. My episode with my mom's nervous breakdown seemed like a distant memory. I loved being at our cottage with my family. There was always so much to do. The park we lived in was called Highland Park and I loved it there. The cottage was great because I could swim and fish anytime I wanted or play sports like football, wiffle ball, & Frisbee. Our neighbor's two houses down were the Hahn's and they would always put out a horseshoe pit and a badminton net up for us right down by the beach to share with all the Hahn kids. We would tear up there lawn every summer, but Mr. Hahn was the nicest man and just wanted us to have fun. He would always play horseshoes with us and none of us could ever beat him except maybe my brother, David, on occasion. We had a favorite water tag game we played called ragtag because we used a rag to tag each other with. Rag tag was a lot of fun because you could hide under docks or behind boats and you tried to avoid getting nailed with the rag.

The cottage was a place of rest; it was an oasis of refreshment and where we could really be kids. When you wake up early in the morning, the lake would be waiting for you with the glistening of the rising Sun. I felt it was smiling at me, inviting me into it sanctuary every morning. It was my abode, as it was for my whole family. Our favorite place to fish was Buckley Point and that was just down the street. When you walked onto Mr. Buckley's property, it was shaped like a little peninsula all around. There was a huge drop-off filled with seaweed and fish. It was such a fantastic place to fish. My favorite fish to catch was called a rock bass because it fought bigger than its size and it tasted fantastic—not fishy—when you cooked it. Years later, we would all watch the fireworks from Buckley point. It was so beautiful because, although we were neighbors, it felt more like family.

When you were at Buckley Point, it felt like we were in another time, like in the 20s or 30s. We would all bring a lawn chair down on the Fourth of July to watch the fireworks. A lot of us kids like to jump on Mr. Buckley's famous hammock, which was hooked in between two trees pretty close to his rocky shoreline of the peninsula. He also had these old cast iron chairs painted white with a bit of a cushion in them. When you sat in those chairs, I swear you could travel back in time to a place that had long passed. Those chairs would bring the time from the 20s and 30s alive again. The breeze at the point at night was gentle and peaceful. That breeze could sooth and push away any problem you may be going through. We all loved going out and taking in the beautiful Gull Lake breeze from Buckley Point.

I remember back then we had such a skinny white dock and my sisters would be out there trying to get a tan. They used poor man's sunglasses by taking a good amount of toilet paper, getting it damp, and making it circular in shape to cover their eyes. Looking back at those make-shift sunglasses, it's kind of funny. You had to be careful on our dock because if you leaned too far to the edge you could fall off into the water.

My mom loved to tan too and she was half Lebanese, so she could get much darker than the rest of us. Mom only used sun tanning lotion, not sunblock, and hers smelled incredibly good. It was Bain de Soleil tanning lotion. And back then, it came in an aluminum tube. The color of the lotion or moisturizer was like a desert orange and it had a smell and a texture so rich I could never forget it even to this very day. Yes, it reminds me of my mother, so it has deep meaning to me. Maybe that's why I still like that color of earth tone orange.

The summer sun made my mom and all of us feel so much better. The beautiful Gull Lake atmosphere was very tranquil with the waves gently rolling in and the gorgeous blue sky above. For sure, it was an escape into a whole different reality. I remember we had a good amount of fishing rods and we would go and get our worms in the forest where there were a lot of wet or damp leaves.

Our favorite spot was just down the street on one of our neighbors' extended plots that had a small forest. The trees kept the fallen leaves sheltered from the sun and damp a lot longer, which were a favorite place for worms to dwell.

Summer always meant high humidity and powerhouse thunderstorms. I loved the darkness of the clouds. I also loved watching the lightning light up the lake and listening to the thunder. Watching storms from the safety of our cottage was great because, even to this present day, I have a strong fear of lightning. There were lots of big beautiful trees in our front and backyard. And I always liked the sound of the wind blowing through the trees, whether it was a windy storm or a gentle breeze; it added to the luster and the peaceful charm of the Gleason cottage.

As a child at the age of 5, life was filled with sand castles and simplicity. I was doted on because I was the youngest. And from what I heard from all the attention I got, I was a cute little guy. Even back then, I remember my mother loved being outside and walking in nature. Everything was homemade and she would make bread, cinnamon rolls and a plethora of different pies. All the berries she put in the raspberry pies were all handpicked from the surrounding woods in and outside of our park. Everything mom made for us came from her heart and it was made from love.

We, as a family, would go to different farms and orchards where we would pick apples, blueberries, strawberries, rhubarb, and peaches. Mom would also make wonderful pies out of all these various kinds of fruits. Many times I would go and pick the raspberries with her, but I didn't have her patience. For me, it was fun for about 20 minutes, but then the summer humidity & heat, plus the prickles from the raspberry bushes would start getting to me. She always used these old yellow peanut butter pails to collect the berries. Mom also made raspberry, grape, and blueberry jam, and it was so much better than what you could buy at the store. All these jelly preserves and jams were put in Mott's glass jars. Whatever wasn't eaten after summer was over would be transferred to our Comstock home in the fall and put on wood shelving in the basement.

Summer also meant different traditional foods we would eat that were unique to the Gleason household. We always had corn on the cob and watermelon frequently with our dinners in the summertime. I remember watermelons were always laid in the water right at the shore of our beach once the water had cooled down to help keep the watermelon cool before we ate it. My dad was the one who would grill the hamburgers or sometimes he would add hotdogs in there too. What was most important to all of us was that we were together sharing this wonderful place we were so fortunate to have. There is so much I can say about every member of my family who I love so much. With all their strengths and weaknesses, faults and character flaws, I would take them all together and hold them tight and never let them go. I will share more about that later. At this point in my life, as I observed all of them, they were all so unique and different.

David, who was just above me, was so good at sports already. He was already excelling in baseball following in the footsteps of Pat and Stevie who were both two of the best players in the area. David was also good at basketball and football. It was these three brothers that I ended up being like as far as sports was concerned. I was fortunate to be included in their practices and it seemed easy for me to catch on to the skills of throwing and catching a baseball. It was fun because they were helpful to me and so skilled at what they did.

Michael, at that time, was going through his old-fashioned car phase. He was obsessed with them and had some small old-fashioned toy cars. Michael used to love holding me under water, pretending he was going to drown me in addition to his evil laugh just before he would pull me under. I was terrified when he did that and when I could get a breath, I said some of the foulest curse words that would echo through the park for all to hear. I would get really mad at him for this. Michael would also splash water on my face repeatedly to the point where it was hard to breathe. He played sports but never got into it as much as my other brothers. He liked school more than most of us and excelled in it. Our neighbors must have laughed their heads off watching us go at it.

Stevie was very much an outdoor kid. He loved to fish, hunt and seemed like an old soul. He used to hang out at the Wessles' house where a very old couple lived behind us. Mr. Fred Wessles mentored Stevie. Lena was Fred's wife and both had a very gentle demeanor.

He was a very positive influence on my brother. Mr. Wessles taught Stevie how to make these wrist and ankle bracelets made of rope and many of us boys and my sister, Gwen ended up wearing them too. The Wessles were beautiful people, for sure. Stevie was very hardworking and good in school. He was faithful and reliable and wasn't a huge talker. Looking back, he really reminds me of my dad with his laid-back personality.

Going in the order of the youngest to the oldest, the next in line is Robbie. At this time of his life, he was into swimming and was an exceptional diver. He was the only one who could do a perfect back dive and he would do it perfectly over and over again off our neighbor's dock (the Kaise family). Robbie was always so much fun to be around and would make up some of the funniest songs. He also was one of the better water skiers in our family. At a young age, he could slalom ski and could spray the water high when he leaned into his turns. I remember Robbie would swim out with this inner tube and had a 10-15 foot fishing line with a worm on the hook. He would float above where the good fishing spots were and start pulling up all kinds of fish and put them in a bag he had tied to the inner tube. I admired Robbie's ingenuity and creative way of reinventing fishing. Robbie was the exact opposite of Stevie and was extremely talkative and social. I remember Robbie liked this one song by the Mamas and the Papas called, "Monday, Monday." He also liked The Bee Gees, Andy Gibb, Elton John, and Dolly Parton.

Kelly was just above Robbie and he was very gregarious and funny in his own way. He loved nature and I remember he had an amazing butterfly collection. Later on in life, he studied birds and got into bird watching. Kelly, even at his young age, was a traveler and helped lead a biking exposition of teenagers on a 100-mile trip to Lake Michigan and back. We had a big picture of all the kids on the biking expedition on our mantle at our Comstock home above the fireplace for years growing up. He liked sports and was pretty good, but his gifts really lie in the arts. Kelly became a very gifted painter and also learned to be a good guitar player without ever having a lesson. Kelly was also into fishing and hunting and periodically would hunt and fish with Pat and Jim Snyder.

When I got into high school, one of his beautiful murals was in my English teacher, Mrs. Kulesa's classroom. When I was little, Kelly would take me out in our little sunfish sailboat and we would just cruise around the lake. I mentioned earlier that I could remember things from a very young age. Well, this is one of those examples. I remember I was a little baby still in diapers and I was right on the sandy shore of our beach. I fell forward face first into the water and I remember how beautiful it was with my head under water... I was at the beach by myself at that time. I was so little that I didn't have the strength to pull myself back up and I was under the water for a long time. Suddenly, I felt someone grab me by my diapers and pulled me out of the water and I let out a big gasp for air. When I looked at who it was that had me in their arms, it was my brother, Kelly. He had literally just saved my life. If it had been much longer, I could have drowned. My mom came running down when she found out what happened and was, of course, hysterical. That day, God, for sure, had sent a guardian angel to look out for me and it was my brother, Kelly. Kelly at that time listened to John Denver. I actually used to sing John Denver songs to my mom whenever she asked me. It was funny because when she asked me to sing it, sometimes I go into our closet and sing for her. She thought that was so cute and would softly giggle when I did that.

Pat, the oldest boy and the unquestioned alpha male, was a very strong and many times intimidating presence. He was very gifted in baseball. Watching him play and pitch, the words violent and explosive came to mind. He would throw the ball so hard that you would hear the ball explode in the mitt. Definitely watching him play was inspiring for all of us younger brothers. I remember watching Pat with the baseball in his hand just tossing it up and down when I was laying in his bed and catching it in his right hand. I think Pat really loved baseball and he knew he was extremely gifted at it. Many of Pat's friends admired his tremendous athletic ability. He was looked up to by many people. We wanted to be like Pat.

He was also an outdoorsman and hunter. All of us boys at one time or another went fishing with him or, when winter came, went hunting with him. Some us got hooked for life on it and others like me just liked being around my big brother. I felt like nothing could hurt me if I was with him. As I said earlier, Pat called me Jamie and that was an endearing name... I felt like the little side kick who could hang out with my big bro on many of his adventures. It was the best to hang with him.

Pat's best friend, Jim Snyder was like Pat—big into hunting and fishing—and I and a few of my brothers would go fishing with them on the docks at night or, even better, we would go trolling in the rowboat to catch the bigger fish. Trolling was where we would cast our lines out the back of the rowboat and let the line go out for quite a ways. The lines had only fishing lures on the line, not worms, and one of us had to row the boat so the lures would drag and have action on them. We usually would go for about an hour to an hour and a half trolling all over the lake. We would catch the bigger fish like bass or pike. So to me, trolling was probably my favorite way to fish. I was close with Pat and he always looked out for me.

Although Pat was tough, I realized he had a soft spot in his heart for his baby brother. He was the only one who took me fishing, snowmobiling (felt like I was going to fall off) and taught me how to catch high pop-ups at the age of seven, which are balls he threw away up into the sky and I had to get under the ball and catch them properly with good form. Pat would stretch me on the baseball field, snowmobile or hunting. He taught me at a young age how to shoot a shotgun. He taught me so many great things and pushed me to perform. Pat introduced me to Soul, R & B, and Jazz music. He played Jethro Tull, Herbie Hancock, Rick James, and my absolute favorite, Earth, Wind, and Fire. I would play them on a record player in the family room on Saturday mornings for years. The album that had a double album with all the pyramids on it. Later on, he got Michael Jackson's "Off The Wall" and then "Thriller." His younger brothers, including me, David, and Michael were influenced by him when it came to watching Soul Train... American Band Stand was cool with Dick Clark, but the dancers on Soul Train were way better. That's what I gravitated towards. Like many people, those two records and Soul Train changed my life forever. I got hooked on R&B and soul music for life. What was cool about being in such a big family was that I got exposed to so many different genres of music because everyone had a different interest.

Now on to all the girls. Our family, by the way, is unique given the fact that there were 5 girls who were born first and then seven boys who were born consecutively. The youngest of the five was Christy. This one was fiery and extremely funny. Very independent and cerebral, she had a voracious appetite for novels. She loved to make people laugh and be the center of attention. During Christmas time, she made up this hilarious dance to the Jingle Bell Rock song and would often unleash it in public just to embarrass us and get more attention. After a while, we weren't surprised when she did this and everyone would be laughing when she was performing. Christy was also a good water skier and swimmer. When she was younger she had buckteeth, so she had to get braces. Maybe that was where all her comedy came from because she could laugh at herself. I don't know why but she used to always ask me if her eyes had changed color. She asked me if her eyes were changing color from blue to hazel green like mine. She always asked it with a little twinkle in her eyes and I just smiled when she did this.

There were two funny stories I heard about Christy. One was where my brother, Pat decided to unwittingly get a small rock and see if he could lob it up and hit Christy. He was so far away, about 300 yards, so nobody thought there was any chance of the rock hitting her. He ended up hitting her in the head and knocking her out. Thankfully, she was OK. To us, it was pretty funny. The other was where our neighbor, Peg Newhouse, had a medium-sized dog named Fluffer. That thing got out and chased Christy down the street with her buckteeth hanging out all the way back to our house. That's the way she described it. And that she seemed to be running for her life with Fluffer nipping at her heels was hilarious.

Rachael, just above Christy, was more of a wallflower and into the arts. A lover of music; I remember she liked Carly Simon when she came out with the song "Your So Vain." She wore that song and the whole record out. Christy and Rachael sometimes went at it and argued at times, but Christy had a much more combustible personality and at times could run over Rachael. She liked to be in the sun and tan too. But because she had lighter skin, she would get burned as red as a lobster. I, at times, would sit with Rachael in the rocking chair and just hang out. In our family, Rachael was famous for one thing. The fact that she could sniff out chocolate no matter where it was hidden. Rachael was definitely a certified chocoholic. Unlike me who loved chocolate too and had a tendency to gobble, Rachael ate her chocolate slowly and deliberately, just a little bit at a time. It was cute how she did that. Rachael's best friend was a girl named Nancy Jackson who lived across the street. They always hung out together. To me back then, they looked alike because they both had long brown hair and were about the exact same size.

Gwen came next and she was quietly independent and a very peaceful person to be around. Extremely athletic and an out-doors woman, she even hunted with a compound bow. Gwen was a three-sport standout in tennis, basketball and track and field. For a woman, she had the strength that I've rarely seen and natural musculature from head to toe. Gwen had a lot of my mom in her, in her love of nature, and amazing creativity as a baker and cook. Gwen was a good diver and would explore the seaweed patches where all the fish were. She told us one time that she came face to face with a huge mamma dogfish guarding her babies. The dogfish chased my sister out of there. Dogfish actually are considered freshwater sharks but only get up to about 2ft long.

She also had a natural ability as an artist. Gwen's painting of Gull Lake hung in the basement of our cottage in our Comstock home for many years even until I entered high school. Here's a quick story about Gwen. When I was maybe three or four, Gwen had a boyfriend named Joe who she dated for many years. Joe was over with his friend, Joel, who was a big guy and we were in the kitchen. Joel took a Frisbee that had a pretty big hole in it and stuck it on my head until he held my arms at my side and I couldn't move at all. The problem was that they couldn't get the Frisbee off my head and I was trapped, unable to move my arms. I started crying like crazy. Finally, they had to get some scissors and cut it off of me. I was scared they were never going to get that Frisbee off of me. With Gwen, I would sit down and listen to her two favorite groups and those were Crosby, Stills and Nash, and the other was Cat Stevens. I loved Crosby, Stills, and Nash and how they harmonized. I felt how they seemed to be one voice even back then. Cat Stevens, the other artist, had such a peaceful voice. As a kid, my favorite song was "Moonshadow." Gwen was an independent free spirit and in some ways mysterious. She was very sweet and loved peace.

Marsha, the second to the oldest, was one of my favorite sisters at that age. Her gifts were in art and she ended up getting a Bachelor of art from Western Michigan University, where I ended up going years later. I used to sit on her lap at the cottage and listen to Joni Mitchell, Judi Collins, and Beethoven while she drank her coffee. The magical spot for this fellowship of siblings was only at the Gleason cottage kitchen for whatever reason.

My sister also served as a teacher/educator, especially to me, David, & Michael, the three youngest boys. She would read *Grimm's Fairy Tales* to me and would often turn off the TV when she felt we had watched too much. She would read to us or have us read if we were old enough. Several years later, the first book she ever bought me was James and *The Giant Peach*. I loved that book. When Marsha gained admission to study at Western Michigan University, she began to take me to movies on the campus. I think they were free and I remember the first one I saw was Flash Gordon. Flash Gordon was the first of many movies she took me to at WMU. Marsha was an artist and loved to paint Murals. She ended up getting her Bachelor of art from Western Michigan University.

Finally, we have Barb, or Bobbie, as we called her, the crown jewel of our family and the Alpha female. She obviously was named after my mom and I say crown jewel because she shined with so many gifts. She was both beautiful and brilliant. School was extremely easy for her; she scored off the charts on the SAT test. Bobbie had an unparalleled love for the holidays, decorating, baking and throwing parties for all of us to indulge in. When I was in my teenage years, Bobbie was crowned the queen of Christmas when my brother, Robbie coined the phrase "Bobbie is Christmas." We all agreed it fit her well.

When she was younger, she loved to lay on the dock and sunbath like all of my sisters. She had darker skin like my mom and could get a nice tan. With such a gigantic appetite for reading, I can hardly ever remember a time that she wasn't reading a book, devouring it from cover to cover. There were a few times I witnessed Bobbie's temper and let's just say you absolutely did not want to mess with her. I remember at this age she called me her little monkey and, once in a while, she would take me to her favorite fast food place, which was Burger King. She could call me anything she wanted; I just liked being with my big sis'.

When I was around six years old, Bobbie ended up getting a beautiful dog named Simon. He was an old English sheepdog. Back in those days, there was a field across from Highland Park where our cottage was and it had rolling hills with tall grass with pathways to run on. We would run back there and play and he would run with us and chase us through all those hills and pathways. Many times, he would give us a playful nip in the butt as he chased us. There's also was a very old rusted metal trough with water in it and Simon would jump in it every time and get wet and kind of stinky. When we got back to the cottage, we had to take him to the lake and give him a bath. Mark, Michael, and I would go back there with Bobbie and run Simon around. The music that Bobby loved came from the era she grew up in. She loved the Beatles, the Monkees, and Herman's Hermits. Groups like that. These are the beautiful characters of my siblings who I shared my life with every summer and all year round.

As I think back, it was wonderful just to go on our regular walks together around the park either during the day or my personal favorite in the very darkest of night where at times you could hardly see 5 feet in front of you. Most of the time the trees combined with the breeze and the darkness, which created such an intoxicating gentle language that you could always feel in your soul and spirit, and you always felt better and revived after a good walk in that park. We have always been addicted to that walk because it always helped ease tension in the house or it was just uplifting in general.

Some of the most powerful walks were with my mother. She always wore these small little flip-flops and she had the most distinguished cadence and sound to her walk. Since she was only 5ft tall, her stride was quick and abrupt. As she moved, those flip-flops would crack over and over. To me, I loved the sound. It was adorable and had a sassiness to it. As I talk of her at this moment, I feel her in me and I miss her. There will never be another like this amazing woman. Everything I did with her was because I loved her so much. I wanted her to always be happy. If she wanted to go for a walk, I never said no. When she walked, she was happy. That's all

I ever wanted for her. My dad would go with us when he got home from work. He was mom's covering and was always there for her.

I have to mention the 4th of July. I loved it at Gull Lake. In those early days, it was so special because fireworks were done right at the Gull Lake Country Club. It wasn't that long of a walk down the beach all across our neighbors' lawns, and the show happened just out from where we were sitting over the water. It was so beautiful as the sky and the lake were lit up simultaneously. Most importantly, my whole family and many of our friends from the park were all there with us. The lake was also filled with motorboats that drove up from all over the lake and we watched the fireworks from a safe distance. My favorite boats were the small army of old wood motorboats that had the most gorgeous gleaming and polished wood you have ever seen along with a roaring inboard engines. Every boat seemed to have an American flag waving in the air, which was proudly suspended at the back of it.

Those were the days. Summer was so special and seemed to go on longer when I was younger. Sailboats with big pluming spinnakers and big cumulus clouds both danced before me like a tantalizing stage play all summer long. Before I knew it, August was here and I didn't want my summer dream to end. Little did I know that my world was about to be shattered.

Wisdom Nuggets

5) Be Thankful and count your blessings. I realize now that despite our family issues, I was blessed with a very loving family and, in that sense, I was given much. Later on in my life as a Christian, I decided to exercise the power of counting my blessings. There was one Bible scripture that helped me with the power of doing this. Philippians 4:8 states: "Finally, brothers, whatever is true, whatever is honorable, whatever is just, whatever is pure, whatever is lovely, whatever is commendable, if there is any excellence, if there is anything worthy of praise, think about these things." One time when I was really down, I decided to exercise my faith and do this. What I found out was that my mental state totally began to change. I began to be thankful and hopeful. My joy actually began to return. It really

helped me to be thankful for the smallest things, like being alive, food on the table and gas in my tank. It was very humbling, but I needed humbling.

6) Proverbs 11:14: "Where no counsel is, the people fall; but in the multitude of counselors there is safety." My family watched out for me, gave me sound advice and always encouraged me. My family was my village that raised me. Without them, I certainly wouldn't be where I am today. I will say this: I have found it very important, as I've gotten older, to watch where I get my counsel from. It's very important to get counsel from people who have experience, success, and a strong level of character and integrity. There are many well-meaning people who can give you a heartfelt advice, but it doesn't mean they are qualified in that specific area to give you that advice. A rule of thumb is to get advice from people who are at the level you want to be.

7) Luke 12:48: "To whom much is given much is required: and to whom men have committed much, of him they will ask the more." I was given much growing up. I had a strong supportive family and successful parents that were pushing me to get a college education. I also had multiple mentors in the form of brothers and sisters and parents. All these people loved me. One of the biggest blessings was that I had two parents who loved each other. Because I was raised in this kind of environment, I have a responsibility to help others less fortunate than me who may not have had the kind of love and stability that I had.

8) Proverbs 18:16: "A man's gift maketh room for him, and bringeth him before great men." There's only one you. Our family, which is made up of 12 siblings, plus my parents, contributed their individual unique gifts to make our lives better in their own unique way. I could never be my brother, Stevie, for example and he could never be me or do what I could do. When you feel like you don't have value, I encourage you to take another look at yourself because with the gifts God has given you, you actually are invaluable.

Chapter 4

Mama's Broken Heart

I had gotten through a wonderful summer and, on August 18th, made it to my 6th birthday. I was ready for my second year of school and greatly anticipating rejoining my friends after my summer sabbatical away. Fall was coming and so was a new teacher. My 1st grade teacher was named Mrs. Murphy. She was a larger woman, but I remember her being very patient and kind. That year, I had to also get a speech teacher because I had a strong lisp. The speech teacher was Mrs. Scott and the Scott family lived just down the street and around the corner from us. I also had an under bite. Looking back, I'd like to think that I looked like an extremely cute baby bulldog. I despised going to speech class because it was just another thing that made me feel less than and behind the other kids in my class.

School was fun and I was already meeting cute little girls and playing fun sports games with all the boys. I also had my own special forces looking out for me, which were my older brothers, David and Michael. The playground was a lot of fun and it had all the standard things like swings, slides, climbing apparatuses and monkey bars. One of the kids' favorite places to go was the small pine tree forest that was on the outskirts of the playground. Quite honestly, it was a beautiful place for kids to explore and to unleash our already burgeoning imaginations.

It was early October and the beauty of a Michigan fall was beginning to manifest. The leaves were turning a kaleidoscope of God's heavenly colors. Soon the leaves would be falling, perfect for young kids to pile up and play in, which was a favorite Midwest pastime. Our regular home on Woodlea Dr. had two maple trees in the front yard that shed an abundance of leaves to play and jump in. We also had one crab-apple tree, lilac bushes and a huge weeping willow-like tree that hung over in the left corner. We would pile the leaves up as high as we could and dive right in the middle of them. It was even better down the street where homes were embedded in thick forest cover. The amount of leaves were much greater and the leave piles you could make were gargantuan.

Fall was a special time and it meant high school football. The maple trees were cool because they had these small helicopter-like things that would fall out of them and we would take them to the football games and throw them so that they would spin in the air. Kind of like our own kind of natural confetti. The Comstock High School band used to play in our neighborhood before the homecoming game. The band and our football teams were always exceptional and everyone in town were excited to go see the game.

Halloween was in sight and I couldn't wait to get my mask. The only store close to us at the time was K-Mart. I remember my first mask was a simple skeleton mask that goes over your face with a simple rubber band on the back, which held it on your face. As a 6-year-old, I loved this cheap little mask so much you would have thought I had just won the lotto. I would constantly be trying it on and putting it back in its little see-through box thinking it would be safer there until I could wear it on Halloween night.

The night before Halloween in the Midwest, at least, was called Devil's Night. That was the day kids would do slightly devilish acts like toilet-papering your neighbors' trees, soaping car windows or egging houses. A few years later, around middle school or early high school, we did all this stuff, but we were too young that year. I remember it rained a constant light rain that year, but we didn't care. In fact, for quite a few years in a row after that, it always seemed to rain on Halloween. I went out with David, Michael, and their friends and was like a little, beloved mascot. It seemed like we were going from house to house with our pillowcases until almost 10 pm. We were on a mission and very resilient on our quest for candy.

There were oceans of kid humanity everywhere in their costumes. Every kid was out there in groups with either their parents or just a bunch of friends. When you are 6 or 7 years old, there was so much excitement in the air. I loved seeing all the decorations and Jack-o'-lanterns that were at almost every home. My favorite place to trick or treat or just walk when I got older was down our street where the homes were nestled in about half a mile of beautiful forest cover and all the homes were set up on top of medium-sized hills. Fall in Michigan had such a distinct and crisp smell to it with all the leaves that had fallen. You could feel the essence of fall way more down in the wooded part of our street. I loved it back then and still love it to this day.

In those days, there used to be candy thieves. They were older kids; maybe middle school or high school age, and you always had to be aware of them. I don't ever remember my parents ever going with us to trick or treat; it was always just us kids. We were never stolen from, but I remember that my brother, Robbie, suffered that fate. He was in our driveway counting his candy in our old blue station wagon when he was hit. I watched them open the door of our car and rip it right out of his hands. My brother fought hard to keep his candy but it was to no avail. The assailants had on ski masks so you couldn't tell who they were. I have the feeling that Robbie knew who they were but wasn't strong enough to stop them.

Halloween was coming to a close and we came home triumphantly with our massive amount of acquired candy. Now the next trick was to hide my candy from my siblings so they didn't eat up my stash. Usually, my brother, Peter found mine because I was never good at hiding stuff. Life was so good. I was on a high and saw no reason it should end now.

Several weeks later, after coming home from school, I was just hanging out at home with my mom and siblings when I heard the phone ring. My mom answered the phone. As I watched her, I saw her countenance change to great sadness. She started to cry. I will never forget what she said saying, "NO!!!! OH NO!!!! OH GOD NO!!!" Then she started to sob uncontrollably. I heard her say the name, Marge. Then I knew something was wrong with my aunt, Marge. I had never seen my mom like this. This was not good... It seemed like my mom was on the phone for a long time. Soon my father was home and there was a big discussion about the events that had transpired.

Later that night, all of us kids were informed of the most dreadful news. Our beloved Aunt Marge had succumbed to a massive heart attack. I learned years later as an adult that Aunt Marge lost some of her substantial estate, which led to her heart troubles and eventual death. After that day, mom didn't seem like herself for weeks. My dad took her to see our family doctor and when they came back, mom just went back to being a mom, doing her motherly routine but she just seemed like her spark was gone.

The next day, mom had a major stroke. When I saw her after that, it wasn't my mom anymore. She was a shell of her former self and she could barely talk. Half of her face and body seemed paralyzed. I just watched her and wanted to help but I didn't know how anymore. She seemed gone too far away from my grasp this time. A day or two after, my dad took her to our family doctor again saying that something seemed very wrong. The doctor assured my dad that nothing had changed and that my mom should just rest.

It turns out that my dad's instincts were correct. My mother's storm wasn't over. In addition to her stroke, my mom was suffering from a major heart attack on that day. It was as if lightning had struck our family. I was so little that all I could do was watch everyone's reaction to what was happening and feel the emotions they emitted. I felt kind of like a little dog who just wants to make everyone feel better. I did know my mom was very sick. I understood this was serious. I was always watching everyone even back then and was trying to see if I, in some small way, could make everything better.

I thought maybe I could pray and it would get better. When I said Our Father and Hail Mary prayers, I started to ask God to please help my mom. Please, God, help her get well. We were trained in our family to say our prayers every night on our knees before we went to bed. We all did. I remember that when I finally went back to school my teacher, Mrs. Murphy, was talking to me about my mom. I remember telling her as best as I could comprehend what had happened to her. "Mrs. Murphy," I said, "my mama has a broken heart." The reason I know that is what I said is because, apparently, Mrs. Murphy told my dad that I specifically said that to her. I was so young then I couldn't fully comprehend what was going on and the severity of what had just hit my mom. I just knew she was very sick and I wanted her to get well. This storm had subsided, but little did I know this was just the beginning of many more to come.

Wisdom Nugget

9) Stand. When all seems lost sometimes, all you can do is stand. I believe that's what my mom did when she had stroke & heart attack. She came back from the abyss of death because she loved us. Like my mom, it's important that you have something worth living and fighting for when life knocks you down. For mom, we were her why and her reason to survive.

10) John 10:10: "He came that you might have life and have it more abundantly." My mom almost died but God brought her back to accomplish her purpose of raising us and being a pillar in the community. That only happened because my mom sought God diligently.

11) Luke 4:18: "He came to heal the broken-hearted and to proclaim liberty to those held captive." My mom's physical heart problems started with having a broken heart about the loss of her sister. God redeemed the situation as my mom both healed internally from the loss of her sister and physically as she quickly recovered from her heart attack. God was in control. My mom always had a heart and a relationship with God, which she periodically would share with us. She spoke of it as if she had a personal experience with him that altered her life path. I remember mom would gently smile and almost glow when she spoke of this experience with God. I truly believe that at this time, when my mom was literally on the doorstep of death, God closed the door on death and said no you can't have this woman today. I don't believe she would have survived if she didn't have a genuine heart for God.

Chapter 5

Healing is in the Air

So my mom slowly started her recovery. Later in the spring of that year, my dad piled nine of us, including my mom, into our blue station wagon and we took 2 weeks off of school driving all the way to Colorado. She was doing so much better by then. Her face started to clear up and got its full function back, but I could tell she was still substantially weaker physically. This was great not only for my mom but for all of the family that attended. David, Michael, Stevie, Robbie, Kelly, Pat, and Christy, including my parents and I went on this trip. It was important so we could all heal.

There was nothing like taking in the mountain air to help heal the soul and elevate your spirit. The trip was fun and eventful. My brother, Michael who was a reader, got a hold of the book, *Helter Skelter*, which is about Charles Manson's murders and was obsessed with it. We all joked about this because this was all he was talking about. It scared me when he talked about the book and just the name, Helter Skelter, creeped me out. My sister, Christy, was fun on the trip, but I, unfortunately, got her mad one time and I suffered her wrath. She grabbed me by the hair and shook my head back and forth like a rag doll. I didn't mess with her after that.

The funniest thing on the whole trip was when we stayed one night at a hotel and we all decided to go swimming in the pool. Robbie decided to be the first one in and did a giant cannonball jump with a huge splash. As soon as he went in, all we saw was a brown nasty plume that went in every direction. Everyone had this disgusting look on their face and then we all burst into laughter. Robbie had not changed his underwear the whole trip and he apparently should have because it all came out in the pool. Needless to say, none of us went swimming that day.

As we got close to our destination, I remember how beautiful it was going through the mountains of Colorado. As we were going up the mountain where we were staying, I remember being really scared because on that mountain, as we circled up, there were no guard rails. If we went off the cliff, we were goners. Once we arrived at our destination, we were all excited... We stayed in this old cabin in the mountains, but we loved it. I remember it had a big screened-in porch and some of us slept there. There was also an extra small house down a little lower on the mountain, which was actually a game room. We never actually got to use that. We were bummed about that.

Seeing my mom enjoy herself in such a beautiful setting made us all feel relieved. She was still able to bake and cook just at a pace she could handle. She had to rest a lot. Sometimes she would just sit outside and take in the bright sun and the refreshing mountain air. I loved seeing that because she desperately needed it. In my heart and in my knower, I intuitively knew she would make it back. We needed her to make it back.

The rest of the trip was so much fun. My dad went on a few hikes with us, but mainly he was looking out for my mom. We went on hikes through the mountains, climbing up on big boulders to get better views. We walked down into the valley and went fly-fishing in the river and even went bird watching and saw a few golden eagles majestically soar above us with total command of the sky. I also remember there was an abundance of beautiful hummingbirds that were constantly coming up to the nectar feeders, which were on the outside of the game room house and we watched them all the time.

Most importantly, we were together and got to share our lives and stories together and create new stories on this trip. The cabin was nice and had screened-in areas, and we played card games at night. I don't remember any television being there, which was probably good for us. To have 10 of us together on such a major trip was something my family never did again but was an experience we all would never forget. The trip was now coming to an end and destiny was calling us all back home.

Wisdom Nugget

12) Wait on the Lord. The bible says in Isaiah 40:31: "They that wait upon the Lord shall renew their strength, they shall mount up with wings as eagles; they shall run, and not be weary; and they shall walk and not faint." Up in that mountain air, I heard my mom praying a few times and I knew she was trusting in the Lord to get her strength back. God truly did renew her strength and she came back strong. It's always good to chase God, especially through praise & worship because in Psalm 22:3, the Bible states that "God inhabits the praises of His people." Doing this is a form of waiting on God. In his presence comes the fringe benefits of healing. So the lesson is to love God, not just when you're in trouble, and he will provide for all of your needs.

13) Psalm 23:2: "He will set you beside still waters and green pastures whose mind is stayed on thee." My mom communed with God when she was sick. I heard her praying. I watched as her healing came swiftly sooner than anyone would've thought.

14) God has a raven in the brook for those who seek him. 1 Kings 1:17 talks of how God sent Elijah a raven in the brook to feed him with bread and meat for many days when he was running for his life from the threats of Queen Jezebel. My mom and the whole family were looking to heal both physically (in my mom's case) and emotionally. The healing atmosphere of the majestic mountains and the soothing sounds of the Colorado were like that for us. When you are going through a rough time, go to God with it and He will give you the rest and sustenance you need.

Chapter 6

The Giver

We got home safely and got back into the routine of school. The Michigan spring was upon us and the anticipation of summer was, as always, uplifting. My mother who had planted flowers just in front of our porch would come out and tend to them. She would give love to them and it was almost like they gave love back to my mother. Again, nature was one of my mom's lifelines. Nature and my mom had a history that went back to her youth. She was healing and step by step gaining strength. This awesome woman had a vision that included not only her children but others who needed healing too.

Bobbie, as my mom was called, was a giver. Not only did she give all twelve of us life, but she gave all of us and many in the community her whole heart. Because of this, she was irresistible. She loved so hard you would swear your loyalty to her. You couldn't help yourself. Back then, I first saw mom begin to help the so-called "less desirables" that lived in our neighborhood.

I heard years later that she grew up this way and learned it from her father, my Grandpa, George. He was an immigrant who came through Ellis Island at the age of 13 from Lebanon. He was only 5 ft 2 inches tall, couldn't speak English and had nothing when he came here. All he brought was his heart and it was a big heart because he became a renowned success with a chain of fur stores that were in the towns Owosso, Flint & Saginaw in the state of Michigan. Some of his brothers partnered with him to run the Saginaw store. Mom was born in 1925, but she grew up wealthy during the depression. She said grandpa used to clothe and feed people who had nothing and she pitched in and helped out too. They, especially, would help the hobos and mom always talked about giving them shoes because they were, many times, walking barefoot.

My sister, Bobbie remembers Grandpa George being very generous at his fur store in Owosso. She distinctly remembers him helping an older black woman purchase a fur coat in the winter for a fraction of its retail cost. He pretty much gave the coat away. Not only that, he loved and talked to this woman for awhile. My sister said it was just how he was. I love all the stories, including this one. I can only imagine what grandpa saw in all these people because he knew what it was like to have nothing, be a minority and had to fight very hard for his success.

My mom had one lady over that I distinctly remember as Hazel. Hazel was an odd lady, an outcast because she didn't smell good and had close to 50 cats at her house. My mom would have her over and just talk to her and love on her. If someone had nobody, my mom would be there for those kind of people. I loved to see the compassion ooze from mom and eventually you would see people like Hazel smile and come out of their protective shell. I could see that she was really just a regular human being who needed someone to show they cared. My mother was that person.

There was one other lady I remember as Peg. Peg was a rather tall, skinny lady who was a chain smoker and a heavy drinker. I saw her drunk a couple of times and I heard that she could curse like a sailor. Mom would have her over and they would always have coffee and maybe a small dessert. When Peg would come over, I watched her countenance change to that of a nice woman. She loved my mom and their long conversations were a healing oasis for Peg and I think this was also helping my mom's physical health improve too.

I was so fortunate to see first-hand my mom's ministry and real calling, which was to uplift people from the darkness and despair and inspire hope through love. She just simply was there for people because she knew they needed it. Mom was the one who was willing to get in the trenches and get dirty if need be to help anyone. I greatly admired my mom for how giving she was and how it impacted these people's lives.

She was extremely kind. I studied my mom and, in my heart, wanted to be like her. It felt good to be kind. These are only two of many people my mom would have over to the house to encourage. Nobody was excluded no matter where you were from or what race you were. I now realize that she was passing on to me and my brothers and sisters what her father and mother had passed onto her, which was looking out for others genuinely and from the heart. My mom wove a beautiful tapestry of home-cooked food, attentive listening and conversation coupled with genuine love for all her guests. She was a product of her parents, for sure. I wanted to be like that and mom, especially, planted that seed in me.

Wisdom Nugget

15) Be a giver. If you're a giver, you will surely have a blessed life. I look at giving as a form of spiritual warfare. My mom was taught by her parents to look out for others and give at a young age. I believe God knew that my mom would have a heart attack and by her helping others heal, healing came back to her. In other words, she gave love and healing to those in need and she received physical healing back. A very powerful scripture in Luke 6:38 of the bible states, "Give and it shall be given unto you, good measure pressed down and running over shall men give unto your bosom." God's blessings include an exchange. Giving is one of God's heavenly currencies.

Chapter 7

Mommy Dearest

Mom was surprising everyone and seemed to be getting stronger every day. Her pace began to quicken in everything she was doing. The kitchen was becoming a food factory like no other. There were 14 mouths to feed. Mom was always making something, whether it was homemade bread, beef stew, or some special dessert. At our house, the food was healthy and mom always took the fat off the meat and did not cook with an obscene amount of butter or salt. Mom ran the kitchen like a general. In other words, she owned it.

She let us help too and we enjoyed learning how to cook. Usually, none of us helped with dinners except when she was making bread or desserts. There was even a news article about mom's baking in the Kalamazoo Gazette and it had a picture of me and all 6 of my brothers seated around the kitchen table with mom in the center of us with one of her tasty desserts on the table. From the picture, I might have been 2 to 2 ½ years old.

As mom began to assert herself in her role, I began to realize that she was super powerful and had a very strong will. She was very involved in every detail of all her children's lives and liked to control things. The tension and conflict in our house had its roots from here. My dad was way more laid back than my mom, but my mother was a confronter. On top of that, she also worried too much. Of course, raising 12 kids was no cakewalk for any parent. When I was a little older, I started to understand what was going on a little better. I saw this pattern begin to emerge, where mom would worry and lament about how the house was never clean and about how we weren't helpful.

It wasn't every second of the day but I could see it wasn't far beneath the surface of her heart. I could tell that we were everything to her and many times she never felt like she was not a good enough mother. She had strong perfectionist tendencies. What she didn't know was we knew she loved us and we would never have wanted anyone else but her to be our mom. She was sad a lot of the time because she put too much pressure on herself.

At the same time, she had a lot of joy too, and her family was her joy. I now know where I got my perfectionism from and it was my mom. There were many times that she would say that we were lazy... Instead of assigning us tasks and chores, most of the time she would lay guilt trips and keep talking about how frustrated she was that we wouldn't help. Many times we would try to help her as she said these words and she eventually stopped talking like that. She never seemed satisfied. She was ashamed of how our house looked and I did not like hearing this from her. None of us did. Looking back, I would have preferred to be beaten a couple of times and be put to work than hear her say that to us. She wasn't at peace.

When this would happen, it brought a very intense level of confusion and tension in the house and could really put people on edge. It was hard to think straight in that environment and many times I just wanted to escape from it. We really weren't bad kids at all, but instead of disciple and order, we had guilt trips, comparison, and disorder. I was told that is called the Catholic guilt trip syndrome. Whatever it was, I wished it would go back to where it came from. My dad tried to run the house but mom just couldn't release control. Dad did assign us kids things to do to help our mom. Even when she would be venting, dad knew what to do and he would pull us aside and have us do the dishes or go fold the laundry. My dad was a great dad.

I remember dad made this breakdown of assigned tasks on a paper plate and color-coated it. It was put up for all to see on our old brown refrigerator. I was excited to see a plan we could follow. I think we all were. For whatever reason, it didn't work for my mom and the plan was not used. I remember being upset about that. We all were looking for order and structure and the plan was simple and crystal clear. I, at the time, was furious that this plan was not followed by my mom. All of us would have rather had discipline, structure and especially the peace that came with it. I know they both meant well and this is just how their personalities matched up.

Our house was more of a Matriarchy.

My mom and dad, at the same time, also never put us down about achieving our goals in school sports or life in general. They were our biggest cheerleaders and always believed in us. They always showed up at all our sporting events, school plays, etc. We had their full support. They expected us to work hard at whatever we did and do it with excellence. Mom, at the same time, was extremely loving and uplifting to us. She listened well as did my dad. I just believe she and my dad had a lot on their plate and was doing the best they knew how.

Even though I really disliked what was happening when there was this tension and confusion, I was willing to absorb it because I simply wanted my mom to not be sad and not worry. My response and meditation were what I could do to break this cycle to see more of the happy, joyous side that I knew she had in her. I remember one time I was able to sit down with her by our fireplace when I was about 12, maybe 13 years old. I asked her questions about what it was like when she was a child. I helped her imagine and dream that day. I wanted to see the person that was beneath the everyday mom I saw.

As she shared her childhood with me, I got her to think and imagine what it would be like if I was back there with her as a friend during her childhood and the things that we would do together. Mom, in detail, began to share what it was like for her and the fun things she did as a child with her friends. Most of the things they did were all outside in nature. When I went there with her, I finally got what I was looking for. I saw her countenance totally change to that of a happy little girl literally full of wonder and amazement. She had the most kind and innocent look on her face. I led her into a dream I conjured up and we talked about the fun things we would have done together if we were both kids and were just friends and not mother and son. We, in our imagination, went past all that was happening to a place of love and friendship. It was kind of like being in an imaginary Neverland. To see my mom with no care or trace of worry on her face or in her spirit was so beautiful. For that brief time I shared with her, mom was free. Actually, I felt free with her. I'm so glad I experienced this with my mom. I will never forget it.

Having been so fortunate to have that wonderful experience with my mom, I was hopeful I'd have more positive experiences with her like that. Mom still ended up going back into mom mode, of course, because we were her responsibility. I never tried to stir any problems up in the house ever because that was already there. That was the last thing I wanted to do. I wanted peace and when the atmosphere in the house was calm, I felt better. When a leader like my mom is desperate for perfection, which, of course, is not possible to attain, it doesn't allow for much peace. Mom, as I look back, had obsessive tendencies. Her passions and needs burned in her. Yes, there was lots of love in our home, but tension was consistently interwoven into our family dynamics.

I started to dream and imagine ways to bring happiness, love and peace into our home. It was something I longed for every day. Not that we didn't have it all, because we did, but there was so much sadness too. Really, the sadness was only because my mom wanted things to match up to her expectations and it's not easy to meet lofty expectations with such a big family. Every situation can't be controlled with 13 other personalities living under the same roof. My God, we must have driven her completely nuts half the time. My mom was not great at being flexible. A lot of the pressure was really what she put on herself from what I could see. Funny thing is, when I grew up, I found out I was just like her -- a perfectionist and obsessive -- and put tons of pressure on myself to just like her. God had to deal with me quite harshly about my own controlling ways later in life.

When my mom would get tense or sad, I did find ways to help her break through it. Many days I would try to help her in the kitchen or go fold the clothes. Mom began to ask me to help her with some of her outreach endeavors. Many days she would ask me to go and give a dessert or homemade bread to a neighbor who was sick to lift their spirits up. These breads were always put in some kind of picnic basket and usually just out of the oven. Sometimes, I didn't exactly feel like doing it but I never said no.

When I helped like this, it definitely made her feel good because, one, I was being helpful and showing I cared. And secondly, because mom was doing something she was born to do, which was uplifting other people. I have to say that when mom got into her gift of loving and motivating, it was something to behold. In conjunction with her worry and negativity, she had an amazing positive side too and was really fighting to make our lives better.

Wisdom Nuggets

16) Love. There were times I really got frustrated and angry with my mom. I hated the confusion and the negative words that permeated our house. Most of all, I hated seeing my mom depressed and sad. I loved my mom, so I endured it. My love was stretched to such great heights and depths. Here is the bible's definition of love and it extols the true power of it. 1 Corinthians 3:4-8 Love is patient, love is kind. It does not envy, it does not boast, it is not proud. It does not dishonor others, it is not self-seeking, it s not easily angered, it keeps no record of wrongs. Love does not delight in evil but rejoices with the truth. It always protects, always trusts, always hopes, always perseveres. Love never fails.

17) Wisdom. The darkness and despair in our house are what got me to desperately search for answers to the problems my family and I were facing. I was determined to have breakthroughs for my mom and everyone else who needed one. The bible speaking of wisdom states in Proverbs 2:4 that "If you seek for her as silver and search for her as hidden treasure, then you'll understand the fear of the Lord and find the knowledge of God." Because I was so desperate every day for answers and remedies, I was on a quest for wisdom. Without the hard times, I would have had no reason to hunt for wisdom. My "why" for the need for wisdom was huge.

18) Ephesians 6:2, 6.3: "2. Honor your father and mother; which is the first commandment. 3. That it may be well with thee; That it may be well with thee and thou mayest live long on the earth." I know not everyone has parents that have been their heroes like mine were to me, but I had times where I was hurt by them also. Looking back, I never stayed bitter with my parents. And because I didn't, I have taken their best attributes of loving and serving others

and have been blessed over and over because of it. I encourage you to forgive your parents and try to learn from their mistakes. Even if they have been terrible to you, by praying and forgiving them, you will break the cycle of pain in the family and protect yourself from repeating the same mistakes they did. Sometimes, we have to be stronger and more mature than the ones that raised us in some instances. I promise you, it's worth it and it very well may change your parents' life forever by you loving them in this fashion.

Chapter 8

Dr. Jekyl/Mr. Hyde & Dad's Retirement Party

So my parents decided that they wanted me, David & Michael to switch to a Catholic school called St. Mary's Catholic. I was about to enter 2nd grade. I didn't know about my brothers but I certainly wasn't happy about the change. This is where I went to church every Sunday, but I didn't know anybody at this school. I remember that the first year we went to church every day and all I wanted to do was sleep in the pew. I tried it one time and one of the nuns popped me in the arm and told me to sit up straight. We were being taught all these Jesus songs and I thought they were cheezy and stupid.

Even at that young age I was aware that nuns had a reputation for being mean and paddling bad kids or whacking them on the hands with a ruler. Also, they always wore their black habits and dresses, so that was intimidating to me too. I tried to never misbehave because I was scared of them and didn't want to get beat up. Soon enough, I made new friends and it was no big deal going to this school. The school was very old and sometimes the big pipes that provided water steam heating would break down.

I found out that some of the Catholic kids were wild and even worse than the public school kids. There were some epic fights on the playground. I ended up making some lifelong friends at that school. I remember that I did get in trouble with my 2nd grade teacher, Sister Marceline, in the first year. I can't even remember what I did, except being guilty of being extremely bored. She wore this old silver cat-eye glasses that looked like they came out of the dark ages and she had a jaw bone that reminded me of my dad's. In other words, to me, she had a manly face, plus nuns wore no makeup and the paleness of their skin was scary to look at. I told my parents how scared I was and, through tears, I begged them to help me out of my predicament. Later that week, my parents were able to get me off the hook.

The school adjustment really wasn't that difficult for me. I still struggled with school but excelled on the playground with the athletic kids. I had very good teachers in 3rd – 5th grade. They really cared, so this may have been a good choice by my parents to have me go to St. Mary's. Our family life still had its ups and downs as always and the same tension-filled atmosphere was consistently present at the house. Thinking back to when we were out of school and at our cottage during the summer, our family atmosphere was way better, more upbeat and peaceful. During the busy time of the school year is when things tended to heat up. I remember that from second grade I had trouble sleeping because I always was anticipating my mom confronting or arguing with one of my siblings or some of them were clashing at the time.

What made these arguments hard was that my mom would never let it die down; she was like a pitbull and these arguments or disagreements most times would go on for several hours. I always felt like I was sleeping on eggshells at night in my bed and I was always afraid of what might happen. I knew my mom was sick, so every night was the same. I would wait up always with a hollow feeling in my chest and in the pit of my stomach and listen for the first intense words to be spoken.

Usually, an intense conversation would begin and eventually an argument would ensue. Then I would wait, praying that it would die down, but most of the time it didn't. It would build and build to the point where voices would be raised and my mom would lament about whatever was going on. I always went downstairs to the kitchen where the arguments always took place and would watch this all unfold. I hated the feeling of worrying about my mom every night. Emotionally, this had to be scary for everyone in the house. That's just how it was though.

When I got into 5th grade, more intense sibling fights began to happen. My brother, Michael was in 8th grade and was insecure with a bad temper. When these fights started to happen and some began to get physical. The arguments kept you up all night. But now Michael would be slamming kitchen cabinet doors or kicking them.

Add to that, now we had full-out yelling and screaming going on. This was the hardest time at our house where I really thought we might lose mom to a heart attack.

This new level of family fighting went on for at least 2-3 years consistently. The worst night I ever remember was Michael yelling at the top of his lungs and finally Stevie ended up hitting Michael hard in the face with everybody watching. Michael started completely going berserk and then Pat grabbed a large piece of cake and shoved it down his throat and into his face to shut him up. Once Pat did that, all hell broke loose. That night, the argument went on until at least 2 am in the morning. There were tears that went deeper and were more far-reaching than what had transpired that night...

Pat was sobbing about something too and never found out what that was about. He always seemed like superman to me, but I found out he wasn't that night. That night, I think was a release for the whole family. And although it was painful to watch, it was real and people were able to let out pent-up frustration and sadness. Our family took a few days to recover from that explosive night. Really, by that time, arguments, disagreements or verbal fights were so common that I was numb to it. Days where people actually hit each other hardly ever happened at our house, but this was the only one where the whole family was there to witness it. If you don't let out what's bothering you, then it's never a good thing. So in that sense, looking back, I'm thankful that our family had that big fight.

It could have been worse, where somebody just gives up on life and commits suicide or overdose on drugs. Fortunately, there was no drug or alcohol problem in our family, so I never had to experience anything like that. Looking back, it was just a huge family having some serious growing pains. For our family, it just was a lot harder because mom was sick. My escape from our family problems was, of course, school and sports. By the time I was in 5th grade, I had already been following in my older brother's footsteps and had played 2 years of little league baseball. I was a pitcher but not a great hitter yet. This is bragging a little bit, but the first game I ever pitched was a no hitter. There were high expectations for me to be great like my brothers and I was trying my best not to disappoint. My teacher that year was Mrs. Hall. She was one of the best teachers I ever had. She knew exactly how to relate to 10-year-old 5th graders... She was tough but fair. She made class fun too and all the students respected her. She was just cool.

I remember one day in the spring it was hot in the classroom and several of the kids had bad gas that day. A couple of kids farted and Mrs. Hall gave us this look. Then someone let loose a bomb fart and she said, "That's it. Everybody outside!" We all started laughing so hard and ran outside for an extra recess that day. Having a great teacher can be life-changing. At this point, I really began to embrace school more and believed I could be a good student someday.

There was a time in November that my dad came home from work one day and was uncharacteristically tired like I have never seen him before. We were excited for dad because after 35 years of working for the same company, he was about to retire so he could be home with all of us permanently. It turns out that somehow the company didn't want him to get his pension. Consequently, my dad suffered a heart attack. He was going to be OK, but I never forgot what his employer did to him. They tried to take his pension away by deceiving him into retiring early and then not give him what he had earned. The other workers at Brown Company loved my dad and demanded that they give his pension back.

At that point, the damage had already been done. On his way to recovery, my dad had to take heart pills to manage his heart condition for the rest of his life. Some nights I would hear dad groan from the pain of taking the heart medication pills. He was really in a lot of pain with the medication he was taking, but it kept him alive. I was thankful we didn't lose him. Later that year, my dad was able to retire and be home with us.

I was really glad that even though my dad retired from work he kept busy. Many times, dad would ask me and some of the boys to do some painting where it was needed in the house. My dad loved helping people and he would do hospital visits to encourage sick people. He was so quiet about his loving deeds that unless someone else told you what he was up to you would never know about it. My dad was a giver. Dad had a laid-back kind and gentle side to him that people were very comfortable with. My dad would ask me to do helpful things around the house, like paint the outside of the house or help hold the ladder for him when he was doing work on the house. Dad was a handyman. I loved doing handy work or man stuff with my dad. I remember he had two hats he liked to wear when I was a little older; one was Detroit Tigers hat, of course. The other was the hat that said Mash on it from the TV show, Mash. When my dad went to work, he dressed very dapper and he wore a very nice overcoat with a wool fedora hat that had a feather on it. We still have that hat today. Dad dressed classy and from another time.

My Dad was a person who always took care of his family and came home every day after work. He could've gotten a lot better job and traveling and made a lot more money, but family was really important to him... It really mattered to us that he chose us first. Dad was great with doing fun things with us, like camping or taking us to the Christmas Kids day at the State Theatre in downtown Kalamazoo. I remember they always played cartoons like Bugs Bunny or maybe Rudolph the Red Nose Reindeer. There's always a Santa Claus down there and we could sit on Santa's lap and ask for what we wanted for Christmas. It meant a lot to us kids when my dad did things like that. I remember dad's big smile and how proud he was to have his kids get a picture with Santa while all the other kids and parents were around waiting to do the same thing. My dad was not flashy; he was a reliable family man and a totally trustworthy honest man.

That spring, I was in my first year in the majors for little league baseball. The two previous years I had played in the minor level due to my age. In addition, I played a lot with neighborhood teams we could assemble. There was a neighborhood field called Hefner Field way down Woodlea Dr, about a mile to the end of our street. The Hefners were a local family that were really good at baseball and had made a baseball diamond on the giant plot of land they had behind their house. My brother, David, was the ringleader. And because he was so good, he could round up much of the top talent in our neighborhood to get a good game of baseball going. Our neighbor, Scotty Dandridge was always there and was very talented also.

He and David always would compete against each other in basketball and baseball, but it was a healthy competition because they were best of friends. My brother, Michael, always came too and was very good friends with Scotty. Actually, Michael and Scotty were the same age and 1 year older than David, but because of sports, David and Scotty had more in common and were a little closer as friends. Sometimes when they were younger, in their elementary years, Michael wasn't welcomed in their little clique and I don't think Michael ever forgot that.

I remember distinctly when it happened and it crushed Michael. They all had made a fort in Scotty's backyard and had made Michael not feel welcome. He came home crying and my mom was there to console him. This was when they were maybe 8 or 9 years old. There was always this rivalry going on since they were very little and Michael suffered that major rejection. Rejection and lack of self-image were a challenge for Michael throughout his grade school and high school years. Later, he would grow out of that phase and finish college and become a successful family man. After this episode, all of us knew that baseball was coming up that spring, so we all had something else to focus our energies on.

So the baseball season came and I had my best season to date. I was pitching better than ever. Our team did well enough and we got to the league championship game. If we win, we get the championship trophy. My coach, Mr. Miggins picked me to pitch in the championship game and I was excited. I didn't expect it because I was supposed to not be allowed to pitch this game because only 2nd-year players were usually allowed to do this. Coach Miggins somehow was able to convince the league to let me pitch. I had been practicing all month with one of my brothers' best friend, Leo Renda, who was on my team. Gameday came and it was very hot that day. We were underdogs because we were playing the best team in the league Party Pantry, but we had a good chance.

The game was very close and I thought we were going to win when Leo knocked a home run over the fence. He ran all the way around the bases and everyone was there to congratulate him at home plate. He was walking back to the dugout and the catcher came and tagged him out. Apparently, he never touched home plate, so he was out and his home run didn't count. I remember I was throwing some serious heat that day and pitching at a very high level. I was striking a lot of people out. I was very confident in my abilities, but

I knew they were the best in our league and I could see they were too. Some of them started getting hits off my power pitches. I liked being challenged. The game was very close, but late in the game one of my brothers' other friends, Mike Lacy hit a home run on me and we lost by a couple of runs. We were all so bummed after losing that game. Oh well, we made a good run at it. It was only my 1st year in the majors; we had next year to win the championship.

Wisdom Nuggets

19) 1 Corinthians 10:13: "There is no temptation that has taken you, but such as is common to man God: but God is faithful, who will not suffer you to be tempted above that ye are able, but will with the temptation also provide a way of escape. He will provide a way of escape, that ye are able to bear it." For me, God gave me an escape from our family trials and struggle with academics by way of sports. I was very good at baseball and it helped my self-esteem. People actually looked up to me because of my skill as a pitcher and, in that way, I was fortunate in the natural. What I didn't know at the time this dynamic was going on was that I was being set up for my destiny as a motivator and evangelist by the trials I was going through.

20) Pain has a purpose. I heard from several great leaders, including my pastor, Bishop Noel Jones, that "pain has a purpose and it's the greatest indicator of where your destiny lies." Dr. Mike Murdock states: "Wherever the source of your greatest pain is, whatever makes you the angriest is what you are called to make a difference in." For me, I hated seeing my family members suffer. Later on, it translated to social injustice and suffering and oppression in the inner cities, which really angered me and captured my heart. If I had never gone through the trials and tribulations I went through with my family, I would never have the impetus and passion I have for helping the less fortunate in the inner cities and hurting people from any background, at large. My calling came exclusively from my pain. I can say that my pain has been my greatest gift in my lifetime.

Chapter 9

Tennis My New Passion

After that baseball season, I just wanted to relax and enjoy the rest of the summer at our cottage. Everything was going great and I was swimming, sailing, fishing, and playing rag tag in the water like we always did. Then one day, and I will never forget this day, I walked into the kitchen and turned on the little black and white TV we had in there. The one with the rabbit ears, and we had put some aluminum foil on top of one of the rabbit ears to help with reception because it was broken. The first channel I selected when I turned on the television was playing a professional tennis match.

The match was between Jimmy Connors, who, of course, is one of the best players of all time and a very good player and arch junior rival of Jimmy's named Dick Stockton. As I watched this match, I noticed there was so much passion and ferocity between these two players that I couldn't take my eyes off it. As the match went on, I found myself rooting for the underdog Stockton and sure enough the match was a nail biter. To my delight, Stockton eked out the match and actually beat Jimmy Connors that day. It was a major upset. For some reason, that match did something to me. I think because they played every point with so much passion, it just ended up reaching my heart.

For sure, I had always liked playing tennis and at our house in town, we had a homemade rack for tennis racquets, which had maybe 7-10 racquets hung on it. We would always go out in the street and hit around or occasionally go to Comstock High School and play on those courts. I also had my brother, Kelly as a big influence because he played on a very strong high school team at Comstock High School. They were the only team from Comstock that ever made the state championships before and that team had a great camaraderie.

For four years, they played all summer everyday together and even rented courts at West Hills indoor club so they could practice during the winter as much as their parents could afford. So really, they practiced all year round. They seemed to have a strong bond & brotherhood and so I was drawn to that energy and passion they were demonstrating. It was similar to what my baseball playing brothers were able to impact on me through their passion and excellence in baseball.

Just two houses up the street is the Cortez family; the whole family was big into tennis. Joe, the oldest in their family, was an excellent tennis player and a phenomenal competitor. He was the number one tennis player on the team and my brother, George, was number 3 or 4 on the team. This team was very solid and everyone could play well. To me, they seemed like super stars.

Soon, Joe's youngest brother, Ronald was taking tennis lessons consistently throughout the year and I found myself begging him to play with me when I was between the ages of 8 and 9. I liked playing all sports, but tennis was always one of my favorites. I also think tennis was just becoming big with names like Jimmy Connors, Bjorn Borg, Vitas Gerulitis and Guillermo Vilas. These were the best players in the world at the time. Watching them on TV, in tournaments like Wimbledon, helped really get me excited about tennis. This era of tennis history was called the tennis boom and I grew up right in the middle of it. That summer, my heart had shifted and I made a big decision. I was going to give up baseball and channel all my energies into tennis. Now all I had to do was beg my parents to let me somehow start taking tennis lessons.

Wisdom Nuggets

21) Jeremiah 29:11 states: "God has a plan for you, one of good and not of evil." My switch to Tennis was something I didn't see coming. Although I wanted to be a top tennis professional in the world, I never got to be as good as my tennis idol, Bjorn Borg. God actually gave me something better and I am now using my skills to teach tennis and other sports to inspire inner-city kids to reach for their dreams and aspire for greatness. Being a positive motivating force

for these kids has become so much more important and fulfilling than me ever winning the biggest tennis tournament in the world.

Chapter 10

Floppy Shoes and the Tennis House

So I was on a mission to start taking tennis lessons like my neighbor, Ronald. I also had my buddy, Jack Wallner from St. Mary's who was taking lessons and was way better than me. During the last couple of summers, I would watch him play against his dad at Gull Lake Country Club, which was a walking distance from our cottage. They would have these epic battles and Jack's dad showed no mercy whatsoever to his son. The matches were always close, but Jack's dad always won. Poor Jack.

I also watched a brother and sister duo, Sean & Izzy Obrien, who were a level up from Jack, and they were amazing players. I loved watching how smooth and athletic they seemed to strike the ball. It seemed like they were in total command of that little yellow ball. These were some of the best players from Gull Lake area, which had a history of having state championship contending teams for high school tennis. Someday, I wanted to be as good as my friends from Gull Lake. They inspired me to want to be a great tennis player, for sure.

That summer, after baseball, I had another defining moment that further solidified my shift from baseball to tennis. My home town of Kalamazoo is where the Boys' 16s & 18s National Championships are played. Kids from all over America come to play in this most coveted tournament. The winner of the 18s age division gets a main draw birth into the US Open Tennis Championships in New York City... A chance to play against the big dogs.

So one of my friends invited me to come and volunteer at the Nationals as a ball boy and, in exchange, I could get in every day for free and watch the matches. That sounded fantastic to me because I loved watching great players anyway. The only downside is that being a ball boy was a lot of work and sometimes the players were not that nice. I, especially, did not like when you were stationed at the net because they had no knee pads or towels to rest your knees on and the courts would get so hot they would burn your knees. Besides me not liking being a ball boy, one benefit was that we did get free coke and lemonade. And best of all, we got to see all the fantastic players.

I remember I was a ball boy for Rick Leach, who became a 9-time grand slam doubles championship winner years later and he was only in the 16s division at that time. You never knew what future champion you may be watching that day. Every major American champion, whether it was Jimmy Connors, John McEnroe, Pete Sampras, Michael Chang, Jim Courier, or Andre Agassi, all played at the Kalamazoo Nationals or "The Nats" as they were called. That summer, all those players battling in the Michigan summer heat and humidity made my switch to tennis complete. It was a done deal.

The Nationals finished in the 2nd week of August. I was so excited to go and play tennis with anyone I could. I usually tried to bug my brother, Kelly first and it was always as soon as we got up in the morning. Kelly was not an early riser like me, so I would try to pull him out of bed and he would use my longing to play tennis to his advantage. It always went like this. He would say, get my shoes, shorts and racquet for me and, as I would be pulling on him and annoying him to get moving, he almost always blows his terrible morning breath in my face. I just laughed; I didn't care. I just wanted to play tennis. If I couldn't get Kelly who was my first choice, I would get my brother, Michael to play, and we were about the same level.

Our neighbor, Kiley Johnson, who had become my best friend during the summer was my other go-to hitter. Kiley was 1 1/2 years younger than me. If we played at the country club, I could only do it after the club house court monitor left because, although Kiley was a member, I was not... Membership to the Gull Lake Country Club was expensive and it was not in our budget to have a membership. When the courts finally opened, I could not wait to hit. Many of the times we played all we had was the moon lighting the court. Those times were special.

That fall, I had begged and pleaded with my parents to let me start taking regular tennis lessons. Finally, they gave in. I was to play at the Kalamazoo YMCA Tennis House where my friend, Jack Wallner also played. I remember I didn't have any tennis shoes, so I had to get some. So where did my mom and dad take me to get my shoes? K-Mart, of course. I could have cared less because all I wanted to do was get on the court. My parents were extremely frugal out of necessity because they had 12 kids, so I ended up getting these no-name K-Mart specials that had absolutely no support to them. I think they cost maybe $2 or $3 dollars, for real. I'm not kidding.

When I got on the court, my friend, Jack, was there to greet me. I was so excited when we began that I ran down every ball I could even out balls. Within a couple of minutes, I looked over and Jack was dying laughing. What was so funny to him was that every time I ran for a ball my cheap K-Mart shoes would smack the court so loud that you could hear it echo off the walls of the YMCA indoor tennis complex. Obviously, I was embarrassed but I laughed about it also. Such was my beginnings as a fledgling and aspiring tennis player. When I got home, I, of course, gently informed my parents that my shoes were not working out. I didn't push too hard, but they got the picture and I was upgraded to some Pro-Keds.

I knew that taking tennis lessons was a big stretch for my parents and I never took it for granted, having the privilege to go after this new dream. That first day on court with my cheap shoes signaled a major change in my life that would end up being a lifelong pursuit and quest for tennis excellence.

Wisdom Nuggets

22) Psalm 37:4 "Delight yourself in the Lord and He will give you the desires of your heart." I don't want to say I was spoiled, but I wasn't afraid to ask for what I wanted from my parents. Being the youngest, I just spoke from the heart and asked... Well, actually, I begged to have tennis lessons. Because they love me, they found a way. I want to encourage you to be bold with God because he says in Matthew 7:7 "Ask and the door will be open to you; seek and you shall find." I have found that if you are bold with him and won't quit, he will give you the dream that is in your heart as long as you have the right

motive. He is a loving God who delights in our success victories and even our prosperity just like our earthly parents do.

Chapter 11

The Coach: Mr. Positive

Coach George Acker (left), Les Dodson (center), and me (right).

I had met Les Dodson about 3 years ago when my brother, Michael, and I took two weeks' worth of group lessons with him. Just doing that meant a lot to both my brother and I. And I could tell even in our brief experience with coach Dodson that he had passion for the game. Les was the tennis director at the YMCA Tennis House and I was looking forward to getting acquainted with him and learn everything he had to offer.

There were a lot of good players at the tennis house. In fact, immediately you walk into the lobby, you could see the list of all the top players down to the weakest player. Everyone who played there was on what was called the tennis ladder. It was a competition ladder and, when I saw it, I knew I wanted to be the best player in the club someday.

Starting out, I really wasn't very good but I liked being at the courts every chance I got.

Besides Jack, my friend, from school who was one year older than me, there were players my age, like Dan Boutell, Jeff Allen, Matt

Benson, Rahul Sharma, Mike Snyder, and Allen Hanson. There were good girl players too, like Monica Earl, Nancy Benjamin, Izzy Obrien, and Betsy Mehaffie. We had 4 indoor courts and 4 outdoor courts. Of course, Michigan winters made it impossible to play outside all year round. So, thank God we had the 4 indoor courts. There were two other facilities in town—Ramblewood and West Hills. They had really good programs but we could not afford to play at two different places. Some of these kids played at the YMCA and some kids played at several of these clubs.

I loved everything about my club. I played 3 days a week, twice during the week and once on Saturdays. I remember my first racket was a wood Dunlop Maxply. Les had us usually playing spread out on the 4 courts and we had walls with accuracy circles to hit into on courts 1 and 3, which we used a lot. Les was a fanatic about hitting on the wall and, especially, hitting into the target. Baseball was natural for me because I had started so young, but I felt awkward on the tennis court because some of these kids hit a solid ball and it felt like it was going to knock me over sometimes. I felt like when I hit with Jack, for example, he could push me around at will, but I naturally embraced the struggle and knew it was only a matter of time and practice until I caught up with him.

Again, I felt like I was behind everybody and I didn't like staying there. This was similar feeling to being behind in school. The only difference was that I felt confident in sports, so I didn't get near as frustrated as I did with school work. Believe me, I was very competitive from the first ball I struck. Even till this very day, I still have the exact same passion and competitiveness for the game. With baseball I felt like I was ahead of everybody but not in tennis. I had some new muscle memory to develop. Fortunately, I wasn't totally unfamiliar and had some playing experience.

Les was good at teaching basic techniques but was a master strategist. He was a former pro tour player who played in the US Open 3 times and won several matches. I remember all his stories and loved to absorb them. He played the number one player in the world, Lew Hoad at the US Open and took a set off the great Aussie. He also worked with the great Pancho Segura, a former number 1 ranked player in the world and who became the coach and mastermind behind Jimmy Connor's success early in his career.

Stories like these motivated me to learn the game and try to be not only like Les but, especially, like the world champions he often talked about. As I watched Les coach, I realized he was a very gifted teacher and he did it with tremendous passion. He also was an incredible player who continued to work on his game. There were nationally ranked players 17 or 18 years old and they were very good, yet none of them could come close to beating Les. With Les, every point had a purpose and there were no free points either. He was the best, he was the chief and an incredible role model for me and all the players at the Tennis House.

Within a year, I started to take private lessons from him. At some point I started to lose motivation, but I remember that my mom sensed it and said to me, "You better get going with your tennis." I never had a problem with motivation after that. The truth was that all my motivation and passion came exclusively from within myself. I was blessed with an unbridled passion for tennis and it never dimmed from that day forward. Once I got it going, it quickly became an obsession.

In Les, I had a kindred spirit who shared the same passion for the game and I did everything he told me to do without question. I was hungry to improve and wanted to play tennis at as high a level as my talent would allow. It later grew into the desire to be the number one player in the world. I didn't care about being realistic; I just wanted what I wanted. Working with Les involved learning proper techniques and then doing massive amounts of repetition to hone those strokes. I remember that once I got the basic strokes down he said, "See how many balls in a row you can hit in the wall circle without missing." He said that the ultimate goal was to hit 500 per row without missing one ball.

Every stroke in the game had a consistency drill to go with it, to see how many you could hit in a row without missing. In fact, there was a whole other board put up that had students who had the highest scores. All us kids who were playing at the tennis house were always looking at the tennis ladder and the consistency board to see who had the best scores or to see who was ranked higher. Both boards were very motivational.

The consistency board had two fitness components to it: 1-minute timed jump rope and a seven-lap sprint, which we did downstairs at the YMCA where the running track circled around the weight room. I wanted to be the best on both boards. And by the time I was 13 years old and 2 years into the program, I began to do all the training from consistency, weight lifting, nutrition, tournaments fitness training and beyond like a religion. I was completely sold on being the very best I could be. I began to play tennis 6 days a week.

I was very fortunate to work with Les because his brilliance in teaching tennis strategy and positive mental attitude were one of the best metaphors for living a successful life that I've ever learned from anybody anywhere. With Les, everything was an opportunity to improve, not a chance to fail. In fact, Les embraced every mistake as an opportunity to learn something. Once you make a mistake, correct it and try not to make it again.

I was naturally a perfectionist and Les knew that. So the following advice was something that helped set me free from my perfectionist tendencies. He said and I quote, "Your goal in tennis and in life should not be perfection, but instead work on doing your best and improving every day. Perfection can never be attained, but improving always can be..." Les was the King of Positive.

Wisdom Nuggets

23) The power of vision. Proverbs 28:8 states: "Where there is no vision the people perish." Les taught with stories and I soaked up his stories. They got me to dream of being a great tennis player. If you are around a visionary, they are very good people to get around. His vision and enthusiasm rubbed off on me.

24) Positive thinking is powerful. Les was so positive and I was so open to that kind of thinking. When I started thinking positive possibility thinking like Les, it was as if the whole world opened up to me. I started to enlarge my thinking to go for being a world class player. And because of that, in the course of my career, I was able to work with some of the best coaches in history. I have also won matches against great players. Granted, it was in doubles, but one of the players we beat in tournament play was a former top 20 doubles player in the world in the 90s. I believe none of this would've happened if I hadn't dreamed big when I was younger and up to when I was older.

Chapter 12

Catching the Bus & the Wake-up Call

That fall of my 7th grade year, my parents informed me that I would have a new form of travel to my tennis lessons. I was to catch the city bus at the end of our street, Woodlea Dr, and go to the tennis house. When I was done, my dad would then pick me up at the Tennis House because by then he was out of work. I didn't care if a pterodactyl flew me to my lessons, as long as I was on court where I loved to be. Now that I had played my first tournament, my dad and I were beginning to learn how the tournament circuit works. That November, I was going to play my second tournament and it was at West Hills. I was told that this was a higher-level tournament much better than the Cortez tournament.

I found out that these kids were highly nationally ranked and as soon as I went into the club, I could see that there was a whole different attitude and energy with these players. They had a cocky swagger and the seeded highest ranked players acted like they were kings of the world. Many seemed to have an air of arrogance about them. These kids were all business and they were serious. The first round I played a kid named David Whetzle. He went right through me like a knife through butter. I think I lost something like 6-1, 6-1. I did not like the feeling at all. I felt like I was at the bottom of the pack.

Like in the first tournament I played, I decided to stay around and watch the top players play. They were much better than what I saw at the Cortez Memorial tournament, for sure. Some of the names I would become much more familiar with or play against later in my career were people like Brian DeVirgilio, Mike Herb, Grant Asher, and Todd Martin. Todd later, when he played pro tennis, became a US Open and Australian Open finalist. He rose to as high as #4 in the world. When I saw these guys play, I realized I had a very long road ahead of me to get anywhere near their level.

I remember I walked by that group of players and the only player who was nice to me was Mike Herb. He was the number one seed in the tournament, so that was a pleasant surprise. He was asking me questions about tournaments that went up to the pro level tournaments and I had no idea what he was talking about. I guess he was checking out what I knew about tennis, which was not much at all. All I knew was that I was glad to be there at this tournament, even if it was to be inspired to be better by watching them play. Mike actually encouraged me that day and didn't make me feel less than. It was a little overwhelming for me because it was only the second tournament I had ever played and many of these guys had started playing tournaments for many years.

There was one match that stood out for me. It was the match between Todd Martin and Brian DeVirgilio in the semifinals. Brian was playing serve and volley tennis even back in the 14's division. When I watched how Todd responded to the attacking tennis Brian was trying to execute, I was simply amazed at what transpired. Todd simply was ripping winners the whole match, whether Brian came to the net or stayed at the baseline. Brian wasn't even playing that bad but Todd continually blew holes in the court. At times, at the net, Brian looked like he had the point won and Todd would hold the shot and then rip a blazing winner the opposite way just out of his reach. I could tell it was very hard to read where Todd was going and that he was an extremely powerful player. Man, I was impressed.

So this second tournament I played was finishing and my mind had new and exciting information and experiences to sift through. I played one or two more tournaments in that school year before summer. The tournament that stood out was another big tournament at Midtown Tennis Center. The club was huge and there were probably over 30 plus courts back in the early 1980s when I first played there. I realized that I was going to take a few lumps since I was just starting to play in tournaments.

I was learning how to get better at tournaments because getting better results would place one in the draw so that one wouldn't have to play a top seeded player in the first round. Again, I got beat soundly by a very good player and I was getting tired of losing. The remaining part of that school year was a big transition for me both in tennis and school.

Mid-year in my 7th grade, I decided to switch back to public school and go to Comstock North East Middle School or N.E.M.S, for short. A lot of my good friends had switched schools from St. Mary's Catholic to other private schools in the area. In 6th grade, I was one of a handful of boys that were in my class. When I got half way through my 7th grade year, I switched and it wasn't easy. I still had good friends at St. Mary's.

When I arrived at N.E.M.S, I was excited because I remembered old faces that I knew from kindergarten and first grade, except they were just a lot bigger now. Some of the good athletes like Russell Moeberg and Ed Brill were still there and they were still some of the best in the school. Friends I knew from baseball, like Troy Rafferty and Greg Witt were there and I became closer friends with that circle. Going to the public school was a much bigger world and I was open and ready to embrace it. I had played basketball in 6th grade at St. Mary's for one year and decided to try out with the team at N.E.M.S. I was descent but only made the B team. I was a little short but I had fun playing and trying to improve my skills on the B team. I liked the school; it was bigger and had more people.

I was the new guy again and it was great to watch who the popular leaders of my grade were. In sports and popularity Russell, Ed, Kevin Jex and a guy named Con Stanton were the leaders and seemed to get all the beautiful girls in the school too. That was ok with me; there was enough girls for all of us. I became friends with all these guys and they were all good people. Con was maybe the best athlete and very well-liked by everybody. What I appreciated about Con was that he was never a jerk to anybody and looked out for people others might reject or look down upon. I thought this guy is cool and had a good heart to go with his popularity. That second half of the school year at my new school, I made a lot of new friends and I was very happy with the decision I had made. I also had a fantastic 7th grade teacher named Mr. Lameer. He had survived an awful ballooning accident where he had received awful burns over most of his body. He was such a gifted teacher and related so well to all of us kids.

What I began to like about my new school was that there were so many more kids from various backgrounds. We had kids that were from much poorer areas and there were those from more affluent areas. We all got mixed together and many became great friends. Some did not and I could see that schools all have their varied tribes. I was actually part of several tribes. I was definitely a natural fit for the athletic group because my genetic proclivities gave me those abilities. These abilities came from my dad's side, dating all the way back to my great grandfathers who were all exceptional athletes and won championships, especially in football.

I was really closer to friends that were not into sports at all and some of them were maybe somewhat nerdy and more into the arts. My friends, Pete DeBruyen, Haley Hawthorne, and Orla Curren were more like that. Orla was actually a year older than me and had older brothers and sisters that were my older brothers' age. Orla was smart and used to help with my school work sometimes. I was very athletic but really a nerd at heart. I was also very close to people in what became the partier tribe. Although I would never become a massive partier, some of my good friends would become legendary partiers. Those friends of mine include David Onderlinde and Todd Rozancavich, among others that I won't name. Those are the two that stood out the most. Well, I probably have to throw Jeff Cooper in there too. We all called him "Coop," for short and he was definitely a partier too. I will not mention all the crazy stuff they did in my book; they will have to tell it all in their own books – which could be something like "Diary Of A High School Party Animal" or something like that. I wish I was more a part of their party life and I may have been just a little envious; maybe just a little of all the fun they had. I was open to be friends with someone from any tribe as long as they were friendly themselves and I had some respect for them. I guess that makes me an extrovert as many people have told me.

There were two adults who worked at the school and lived on our street. Mrs. Maitland was the school librarian and Mrs. Large was the home economics teacher. I got caught once by Mrs. Large eating peanut butter with a giant spoon once. I was so hungry I couldn't help myself. I guess I wasn't sneaky enough. She just looked at me and verbally scolded me; kind of gently actually. I thought I saw a little smile on her face too. Probably so because she was friends with my mom.

I was very happy at my new school and it gave me a good balance to complement all the tennis I was playing. That year, I also began to work harder on my tennis and coach Les told me there was an important tournament called the Qualifier. He said I should play. He explained to me that if I could do well enough in this tournament I could qualify to play in the sectional tournament in Indianapolis. Doing well enough in Indy meant I could then qualify for the national 14's tournament. I ended up not playing it my first year in the 14 and under. Instead, I played the Cortez Memorial again because I didn't feel like I was quite ready to play the Qualifier.

That summer, I ended up winning a few rounds at the Cortez tournament. My third round match, I remember, I was so inexperienced that I brought orange juice to the match to stay hydrated instead of water. It was very hot outside and, instead of finishing the match, I threw up and had to default. I was very disappointed at that result but I knew now that I had improved quite a bit from the previous year. I was winning more matches and gaining experience. Again, that summer, I played about three more tournaments, plus the inner city matches against other clubs and began to get accustomed to playing matches. Slowly, I was becoming a descent tournament player. It was a process. It felt good that I could compete and not get blown off the court. Really, my tournament journey was just beginning.

Wisdom Nugget

25) Losing can actually be winning. When I lost a match or studied hard for a test and did bad or even got an F, it ended up being one of the best things that ever happened to me. I remember studying for a science test in 7th grade diligently for 6 weeks. I was hoping to get a good grade but instead I failed the test. It hurt so bad that I literally cried and I very much felt that all the hard work was for nothing. Desperate and not wanting to ever go through that again, my parents talked to a counselor and they recommended a learning program

called, "If There's A Will There's an A." I eagerly went through the program and learned about a learning tool called mnemonic devices, which help you remember definitions and answers to questions much easier. After failing that test, I began to improve my scores much higher after that because of the new learning strategies I had acquired. I even later on got two college degrees and I used those same skills to get through college too. Losing a tennis match always has got me to assess myself and put a fire in me like nothing else could to find new ways to improve my game. Never quit in life and always fight back. Only when you quit in life do you truly lose.

Chapter 13

True Commitment

That August 1983, I had just turned 13 and was headed into my eighth grade year. Les and my dad had been talking and my dad made it clear that I wanted to totally commit to becoming a serious tennis player and go as far as I could. I was already bugging Les and my dad about it anyway. To do that, I needed more time with Les and that meant more private lessons and more group lessons along with tournaments and proper training.

After the conversation, dad said we had some good news. Les had connections with the sponsor called the Kalamazoo Tennis patrons and they were going to help pay for my lessons to make them more affordable for us. When I found out about this I was extremely excited about this new development. I was just a kid with a dream and I began to throw myself into the game and every dimension imaginable. Les recommended a book called *Tennis For The future* by Vic Braden. I used to read that book and try to copy what it said to do exactly. Les said a good way to perfect your forehand is by doing three-form swings a day in front of the mirror on every stroke, so I began to do it every day.

He also said that to get physically fit you need to get a proper weight lifting program and that was put in place. We did and I did it religiously 6 days a week. I started additionally pursuing the use of mental training and I found it very beneficial. The first book that I ever used for mental training was called Mental Toughness by Dr. Jim Loehr. I had found out later that he was the mental toughness coach at Nick Bolleterri's Tennis Academy where many of the top players from my generation were training at the time in Bradenton, Florida. And his training was very helpful with things like visualization and retraining your thoughts to be positive so that you get rid of negativity and bad self-talk when you're playing.

I even learned to visualize whole matches and patterns of play before I played them. This ended up helping me stay more focused in matches, especially when I got into college and practiced visualization more. I also studied fitness drills from books like Martina Navratilova's fitness training book and I got fitness drills from there. Les also set up fitness drills for me, like one-minute jump rope, seven laps, which was a two-minute sprint. I did long-distance training probably longer than I needed to, up to like 6 to 10 miles for endurance during matches. I also did lots of agility drills like plyometrics, suicides, and shuttle drill, which I ran between the service and a baseline for 30 seconds. I wanted to be fitter and faster than anybody on the court and I pursued that goal diligently throughout my career.

Les always talked about how fit the Australians were and there was a great coach named Harry Hopman, who trained them physically to be the fittest tennis players in the world back in the 50s, 60s, and 70s. I also got into nutrition a lot. I found out that eating red meat before a match was not a good idea because your body couldn't digest it quickly and it would tire you out before a match. I ate things like pasta, chicken, fish and lots of green-leaf vegetables. Martina Navratilova co-wrote a book about fitness and nutrition with a guy named Dr. Robert Haas. It became the hottest book of the time. All of these different areas of tennis technique, physical fitness, nutrition, and mental training were components that I began to delve into and began to repeat religiously.

Les told me to keep a diary of all my fitness and consistency trainings. I still have that diary with all of my fitness times and records and consistency records that I had from age 13 age 18. I found that Diary was a good way to track my progress. That year, I played several tournaments in the fall and in the spring, I was getting ready to play the qualifier in Grand Rapids, Michigan for the first time. The goal was to do my best there and hopefully qualify to go to Indianapolis.

As I was working all these components of becoming a high-level tennis player, I began to realize that I wasn't like a lot of the other kids. I was truly obsessed with my goals. This was all I really wanted to do. As I got into more tournaments and more competitive at the club, I began to clash at times with some of the people at my club. As I started to win more, I lost a few friends. I was on a mission to be a great player and my passion rubbed some people the wrong way.

I wasn't loud or arrogant with how I acted on and off the court, but my passion was always evident. Some admired it and others didn't like it so much. I always felt like I was from a different place, a different world than the other kids around me. I was always attached deep in my heart to what was going on in our house or trying to be a top-level tennis player. Chronologically, I was 13, but in my soul and spirit, I was much older. I was very driven. I was a treasure hunter for wisdom and looking for a way to help my family have a brighter blessed future and also trying to get new information or coaching that could get me to the next level as a tennis player. I didn't understand how to let go of what unfolded at home. It was always with me and not far from my heart and mind. I was a hoper. I had to have hope and tenacity to get through my family issues and to also reach my ambitious goals as a tennis player.

This would be my second year in the 14's division and first time to have played in the qualifier. When I finally got to the qualifier that June, I remember the people I saw at the tournament that fall; people like Todd Martin and Grant Asher, who still had that attitude and swagger that I remember from the fall tournament. They acted like they expected to win. There's also another player there who was the number one seed. His name was Damon Valentino and he had that same attitude. I remember seeing him in the Western Michigan WMTA yearbook as the number one player from here and was in the 12's and 14's division.

There were also some other players in Kalamazoo who were very good too. One of them was Bob Borski and the other was Rob Vandenbrink. I remember Bob was very smooth and had good ground strokes and Rob was a power player with a huge forehand. I knew he was very dangerous watching him play. There was a handful of good players from Kalamazoo and none were from my club in my division, but instead, they were from West Hills and Ramblewood tennis clubs. The majority of the really strong players were from Lansing. I saw Todd Martin and Grant Asher playing in the qualifier and I knew this tournament was important.

I ended up, I guess, losing the first or second round. But just like I did in the previous tournament, I stayed around to watch these players who obviously had been playing for many years longer than I had. I remember this one match between a top player from Lansing and a kid named Jason Given from the same club who was a very good left-hander. He seemed to have fun during the match because he kept saying yeah or nay during the rally, like he had total control of whether he lost each point and he acted like he owned Jason. Some of the other kids were laughing and I didn't think it was that nice to be acting like that. It pretty much humiliated Jason and he ended up losing this match 7-5 in the 3rd set. I felt kind of bad for him.

In the quarterfinals, Bob Borski played Damon Valentino and I could tell Bob didn't believe he could win and he got beat in straight sets. So in the semi-finals, I watched Damon Valentino play Todd Martin and Todd looked like the best player in the tournament. I also watched Rob Vandenbrink play Grant Asher in the semi-finals. All these players had already qualified for the Westerns by winning the quarterfinal matches, which was in Indianapolis at the time. In the semi-finals, Grant Asher got overpowered by Rob Vandenbrink in straight sets. Todd Martin ended up outclassing Damon Valentino. I could tell Damon was really mad about losing that match.

I really enjoyed watching the finals where Todd Martin beat Rob Vandenbrink in a good match, but Todd was simply better and more polished. No matter how hard 'Rob hit the ball, Todd hit through it even harder and could hit corner to corner with rocket-like power and tremendous accuracy. I was really impressed and I could see that Todd would eventually become a great player. He had that look about him. At the qualifier that year, I realized I had my work cut out for me because I was behind a lot of these players; they had been playing tennis much longer. I knew I wanted to be a part of the pack of really good players who were serious about tennis, but I wasn't there yet.

I couldn't wait for the Cortez Memorial tournament, which was my second time in the tournament. I worked on everything I could, from fitness, stroke consistency, match play and weight lifting in preparation for the tournament. Les was also beginning to teach me basic patterns of strategy and percentage play so I could begin to limit my errors and quit beating myself in matches. This year, I was more ready to excel in the tournament. I worked hard on all areas of consistency, including wall work and was starting to hit over 50 or more shots in a row without missing, including volleys. Les promoted developing an all-court game and building consistency so that all my shots could stand the pressure that comes with the competition.

At that tournament, I realized that I had some things working in my favor. One, I enjoyed running for every ball and getting it in play. Secondly, practicing consistency was paying off and I wasn't missing that much. Finally, even though I was only 13 years old, I was comfortable volleying at the net and was winning points up there. I felt like I was getting pretty good at making my opponents have to beat me while striving to not beat myself. Les always stressed that.

This year, I was able to get all the way to the semifinals of the Robert Z Cortez Memorial tennis tournament. I had accomplished my first legitimate breakthrough in competition. I played one or maybe two tournaments for the rest of that summer, but it was this one that stood out. I did not work at the USTA Nationals that year but was able to watch some amazing battles unfold that year. The 16's division had one player that stood out from the rest and that was Aaron Krickstein. He absolutely ripped the ball, especially his forehand and seemed to be extremely mentally tough. I was mesmerized by how he played more than any other player in the whole tournament. In the 18's division, it was very exciting and a very low seed by the name of John Letts ended up winning the tournament. It was very much unexpected. With the fresh inspiration of The Kalamazoo Nationals in my sails, I was ready to have fun and work harder than ever to be a qualifier for the Indianapolis Sectional tournament next year. It was going to be a great challenge because I was moving up to the 16 and under division now.

Wisdom Nuggets

26) Hard work brings favor. At this time in my tennis career, I started working hard on every area I possibly could. I worked on mental

training, weight lifting, speed/agility training, tennis technique, and strategy. I did it with passion and my whole heart. My hard work began to get noticed and I believe that is why favor came my way to get sponsored by the Kalamazoo Tennis Patrons. If you go after what you love with your whole heart and are very persistent, the doors of opportunity and even abundance will eventually open for you. In proverbs 12:24, it says: "The diligent shall prosper (bear rule)." That's what happened for me.

27) Stay in the game and keep on fighting. At that time in my life I had lost in the qualifier and was momentarily disappointed. My attitude was that I lost one battle but I hadn't lost the war. With my goal and dream firmly entrenched in my heart, I hung around to learn and grow by observation. The Passion and dream grew every time I was near a tennis court. My journey started with those first few steps, which included me getting whipped in the beginning. Later on, by being persistent and passionate, the tables turned for me. I began to move up the rankings and beat people who used to beat me easily.

Chapter 14

Funny Family Stories

Now I'd like to transition to some of my favorite family stories. Just before I got into tennis, I had another passion and it started in my 4th grade when I got into raising pigeons with my big brother, Pat. Pat and I had to make our own pigeon coop, but we had to get the wood and equipment first. Pat came up with a great idea to go down the street where they had plywood at houses being built and steal it, which was the cheapest route to making a coop. So at the age of nine I went with my brother, Pat and grabbed pieces of huge plywood at night down around the block from my house, which was about half a mile, and walked back down to our house carrying this above our heads. I was concerned we might get in trouble for it, but it was pretty late and I trusted my brother over my fears. Needless to say, we had all the wood we needed for our first pigeon coop. That was just the beginning of our criminal activity.

The first pigeons we got were from Jim Snyder and what was cool about the birds was that they would flip in the air and sometimes they would spin down 40 or 50 feet before snapping out of the spin. We also were looking for better birds to breed and a few times snuck into other people's coops in the area and stole a few birds. The ones with the red bands around their feet were the best spinners. One day after stealing some birds, Pat and I tried to sneak into the basement without my mom finding out. As soon as we opened the door to go to the basement, the birds started flapping their wings very loud in the paper grocery bag we had them in and my mom heard it. My mom said, "What have you got in the bag, Jamie?" I said, "Nothing, Mom!!!" and went down the stairs. Mom knew we were up to no good but never pushed the issue. I had never stolen anything in my life but I decided to trust my big brother. I wanted the wood for the coop and those birds probably more than Pat. I really was obsessed with pigeons for about 3-4 years.

At this time in my life, I really enjoyed hanging out with my brother, David and one of his best friends, Brian Schmitt. Sometimes people called him "Schmitty." David's nickname for him was "Worm". Brian became like our 8th brother. I remember my mom had a really good motherly connection with Brian. She totally included him as part of our family. I think she knew innately he needed this inclusion and love. Brian brought something to the table that you don't see every day. He was loud, hyper and completely nuts at times and that's why we loved Brian. If he was over, he was going to be on center stage a lot of the time and you would be laughing your butt off at some of his antics. It was hilarious to see Brian mess with my brother, Pat. He was a skinny scrawny wrestler and he would jump up on Pat's back and neck and hang on him like a barnacle on a boat. Then he would start trying to slap-fight with Pat. It was funny.

I will never forget how, down in our basement, some of my brothers, along with Brian, decided to see if farts were flammable and got a lighter and started to try to light their farts. Well, after countless attempts, one caught fire a little bit and we started to laugh. My brother, Stevie conjured up the most vile, disgusting fart imaginable and tried to light it. It was definitely silent but deadly. And when he lit that, it looked like a small flame thrower. We all laughed like crazy but Brian went berserk. He had these high-pitched screams of laughter that echoed through our basement and kept going about it for several minutes. It was funny though.

Another super funny story was back when my brother, David was in middle school at St. Mary's Catholic and the nuns for the first time bought a small dog named Lochi. David and his friends used to pick on that dog a little bit. Sometimes Lochi would go poo in the school and students would have to clean it up. It was no big deal though. One Christmas around that time, David and Brian decided to get my sister, Christy a small present that year. She was excited and started to open the present while she kept asking what it is. As she fingered through the present, she said, "What is it? Beef jerky?" And none of us could control our laughter any longer as David blurted out "NO, IT'S LOCHI TURDS!!!!!!" We all literally started rolling on the floor laughing. Christy was laughing too but pretty grossed out at this prank they had pulled on her. It was hilarious that Christy had been tricked into thinking that this old, dried out doggie pooh was beef jerky.

We had tons of fun as kids. Some of what we did could have gotten us in pretty big trouble with the authorities. Somehow, my brother, Pat was able to get a hold of some golf cart keys from a local golf course and a bunch of us brothers, including Schmitty and some other neighborhood kids went riding on those golf carts all over that golf course that night. We were going off the edge of steep hills at high speeds doing jumps with them. We even rolled one over a couple of times. Luckily, nobody got hurt. Was it slightly illegal? Of course, it was, but it was a night of fun none of us would ever forget.

Here's one unique story that I'll never forget. When my brother, Kelly was in 6th grade, he was getting picked on regularly by a bully who used to steal his lunch every week. Finally, Kelly had had enough and decided a plan to get back at his oppressor. He was going to put an added special ingredient into his peanut butter and jelly sandwiches that might not taste so good. Sure enough, the bully returned the next day demanding my brother feed him another free lunch. My brother willingly gave up the lunch as usual so he wouldn't get a beating. This time, the bully bit into the PBJ, but there was quite a bit more crunch than usual. My brother had put mealworms in the sandwich and they were now in his mouth. He chased Kelly all over the place but never caught him. Needless to say, Kelly never had a problem with that bully stealing his lunch after that.   I remember between the years of 4th through 6th grade a lot of my brothers and sisters were still at home going through college... I have fond memories of this time because we did so much together. When you look out through our front window, you could easily think that our driveway and the cars parked on the street looked like a used car parking lot. My brother, Pat had three cars; one was a very nice convertible VW bug white with a black top. The other two were not so nice. There was an old early 70's light brown convertible Corvair and the crème de la crème of ugly cars—an orange and rust Dodge Opal. He bought that car for $25 and I don't know if it was worth that. Maybe it was worth it because it did start, but its top speed was maybe 35 miles per hour. Everyone had a laugh about that car.

Stevie also had two cars and these choices of vehicles magnified the fact that my family had some eccentric tendencies. The first car was a bright yellow VW convertible Thing. I loved that car; it was pure fun. The other was a dark brown Studebaker and it was huge. I had no idea how old that car was. I think he had that car for maybe a year and got rid of it. I think Stevie and Pat were competing to see who could get the most outlandish car. My sisters, Christy and Joanna, both had Subarus at the same time; one was green and the other was blue. My sister, Gail, being the outdoor type, always had an older VW bus.

What I love about these cars is that they say a lot about my family's personalities, but even more about their characters. None of them were followers, but they were just themselves and did things their own unique way, whether people understood or accepted them or not. To me, they were free; free to be themselves and comfortable to not put on any fakeness or any kind of mask. In other words, with my family, what you see is what you get. What was cool is that being from a big family, I not only had my own stories but got to be a part of my siblings' stories.

One of my favorite all-time family stories happened fairly frequently actually and it was in a place where my mom would frequent -- the kitchen. This is exactly how this would go. Mom would be getting on our case about something, maybe even voices were getting pretty loud between my mom and one of us kids and all of a sudden the phone would ring. Mom would say super loud, "EVERYBODY BE QUIET!!!!" And of course, we were quiet, kind of. As soon as mom started talking on the phone, she would totally change her tone to sound like the sweetest little angel and say, "Hello Gleason residence" all the while looking at us with daggers in her eyes and this look on her face that said she was going to strangle us. We would go in the other room and start kind of snickering with laughter every time she did this.

One other time, it was late and my brother, Stevie and I were in the bedroom next to my parents laughing and keeping our parents up. We just couldn't stop laughing. They were just little laughs but enough to keep them up. My dad said, "Would you guys cut it out?" but we kept on any ways. Then mom said, "We're trying to sleep.

BE QUIET!!!" For a short few seconds, we were quiet but then we couldn't help it and then we let out a few more little laughs. That was the last straw. All of a sudden we heard our mom get out of the bed and started stomping over to our room. All of a sudden the door flew open, the light was turned on and mom said in a high pitched shrill, "Oh you kids!!!" and comes right for us. Her eyes were a little bit bloodshot. She grabbed my hair and shook my head back and forth like a ragdoll. It didn't hurt at all and Stevie and I were a little stunned. As soon as mom left the room and slammed the door, Stevie and I looked at each other and just started roaring again with laughter. That was the end of it though. After that, we quit so mom and dad could get some sleep. Stevie and I named that hilarious family episode "Dance of the baby elephant" because of the way my mom stomped over to our bedroom to come get us. That was the best.

In 7th and 8th grade, I used to have friends come over and stay the night for Devils Night and Halloween. My mom would make pancakes in the morning with maple syrup every time. My friends, Kevin Herwick, Scott Henby, David Onderlinde, Greg Witt, Troy Rafferty, and Todd Rozankavich would all come over. On Devils night, we would be out messing around, toilet-papering people's trees and egging houses. No one ever caught us, but it was an adrenaline rush for us.

We also went camping a couple of times together back in the wilderness behind H Avenue, which was one street down from our house on Woodlea Dr. We pitched our tents in the pine tree forest back there in case it rained. Of course, it did rain the first time we went out. I remember I made up this stupid song about my dog whose name was Bonkers, who my brother Kelly had named after the dog in a Robin Williams' movie, "The World According To Garp." The song was so bad, but everyone was laughing their heads off. We had a blast and felt like kings of the world. My friends were nuts; I don't think I have ever laughed so hard in my life. We also had our fishing rods and went fishing in the stream, which was maybe half a mile away. When you are 12 & 13, we were all just beginning to get into girls, so there was innocent and sometimes not so innocent guy talk going on. I remember we had a Playboy and Penthouse magazines we all looked at. We thought we were pretty cool.

We had to buy a lot of our own food, which included hot dogs, Kit Kat candy bars, Eminem's and, of course, we made s'mores with marshmallows, Hershey's chocolate and gram crackers. There was a movie called "Stand By Me," which was about 12-year-old's who went on a long camping hike to look for a missing kid their age. Although our hike wasn't close to as long as in the movie, I can attest that we experienced many of the same things those kids experienced. We told stories, we dreamed dreams and we felt invincible. Just like the movie stated, those were some of the best times of our lives, and some of the happiest. None of us will ever forget them. My middle school years had come to completion. Now high school was awaiting me.

Wisdom Nuggets

28) Laugh and laugh some more. Although our house had many tense moments, there were so many characters. In my giant family, we knew how to have fun and be crazy in a good way. In our house, extra laughter was needed so we could release unhealthy negative feelings and emotions. Now that I have gotten older and living in California, my good friends have gotten me to a point where I'm actually laughing hearty belly laughs quite regularly. I don't think I've ever been happier in my whole life. I just recently started looking at myself and realized that growing up, laughing didn't happen that often for me. I've noticed that I am finally walking out of the shadows of my past. I'm not that same kid who was constantly worrying about his mother or other family members. It's almost like my new laughter is breaking up the wounded areas of my heart. I have heard the saying that laughter is the best medicine and for me, now that I am really experiencing it much more often, it has really proven to be true for me. I do have to say that in the last couple of years, I have gotten around some great quality people and separated myself from some very negative ones. That has been the biggest key to my new found laughter. I call my new crew that I hang with "The No-Stress Express."

Chapter 15

High School Years & the Journey to Indy

That fall, I began to work extremely hard on every area of my game. I got faster and stronger, more consistent, and played more tournaments. I was also going into my first year of high school tennis. I remember my friends from Gull Lake High School wanted me to play on their team. They were very good and went to the state tournament every year. I thought about it and decided to stay at Comstock High because I knew I could most likely play number one there every year and that would be great practice for me. Every day during lunch, I would do extra wall work and hit into the wall target. Eventually, I got permission and a key to come in and do extra fitness in the high School gym and Ms. Ashby, a long time gym teacher and family friend, gave me extra fitness drills to do, which I eagerly embraced.

On the Comstock High School Tennis team, we had a teacher named Mr. Gardner who was a first-year coach. For years, the tennis coach was a teacher named Mr. Stickle. Now he had taken the Athletic Director position. I knew Mr. Gardner from being a middle school science teacher and all the students liked him. When practices began, the upper classmen put me in check right away and made sure I wasn't too cocky. I understood my place and just rolled with it. Eventually, I was accepted as one of the guys. I liked our practices because Coach Gardner did a lot of fitness drills like running through the halls for about 30 minutes straight and agility drills.

We also did lots of hitting drills and matches. Some of the older guys, especially on the team, made fun of the drills and the running, but I didn't really go with that in my heart. I just kind of went along with it a little bit. I think it hurt Mr. Gardner's feelings. He was really a good guy, an honest guy. My first year on the team was with a good group of guys and we had a lot of fun. Our upper classmen were juniors; we had no seniors on the team that year. Jerry Bastian, Coleman Large, and then our sophomores were Clint Fleck, Rob Baird, Matt Keenan, and Steve Bell. I was the only freshman on the varsity team. We had a lot of fun at practices and at the end of practice we were allowed to have what was called a ball war. We would whack balls at each other from across the net and we all got tagged pretty hard sometimes. I distinctly remember Rob always yelling out, "Ball War!!!" and then balls would start going through the air at supersonic speeds. It probably would have been a good idea to wear a helmet when we played this game.

During high school, I had a lot of friends but I didn't get into a lot of the things they did because I was so committed to tennis. I was a tennis player pretty much and that was about it. My friends would be partying and many drinking. I never drank at parties and neither did my brother, David. It had a lot to do with how we were raised. I didn't want to do something just because everyone else was doing it. The opinions that mattered most to me were of my parents and my brothers and sisters. They were who I looked up to more than anybody. I was well-liked by most people, but I never felt like I fit in with everyone else. When I went to parties, it felt weird and uncomfortable being pretty much the only one who wasn't drinking. Everyone was cool and respectful to me even though I was choosing a different path. I think they respected that I wasn't a follower and trying to do what I thought was right. As a driven person on a mission, sometimes it can be very lonely when you are that person.

During high school, I had fun with playing basketball in my freshman year. I didn't start and I was vertically challenged at the time. We had fun and a good bunch of guys on the team traveling to games and just being goofy knucklehead kids. We had this big guy, Grant Cook, who would play this song, Bang Your Head by Quiet Riot. During certain parts of the song, he would bang his head on the school bus seat and we would all be dying laughing. Some of us were concerned Grant would get brain damage from his antics. He was smacking his forehead on the top of the seat pretty hard. LOL!!! We had fun on our trips and had a pretty good team too. When I started high school, I became more committed to my tennis and became known as the tennis player. I sometimes would go to parties with my friends, but mainly I was at the tennis courts getting ready for my future of being a college tennis player. To be a top college player or maybe even a pro player took total commitment and I think my friends understood that.

As I got into high school and my brothers, David and Michael, started to mature, there was a lot more peace and fun in our house. There were still some tense times, but they were getting less frequent. We were the only ones in high school and everyone else was either in college or had already finished. With less people there, it was easier for my mom and dad to manage. A lot was happening. We were not the only three at home. The older siblings for short or maybe even fairly long stretches of time would come home to live. Even as family members were moving away, I was always watching them from afar and missing them. I'm still the same way till this very day. My heart will always be connected intensely to all of my family until my last breath on this earth. Part of me back then would want them to live in Kalamazoo so I could see them whenever I wanted. At the same time, I was also very happy that they were living all over the country and eventually the world, having an exciting life. Distance never limited my closeness to them.

I remember when I was 10 and my sister, Christy, was moving away to California. When she was leaving that day, I broke down crying and sobbing. Since I was little, I was always the happiest when we were all together. And when Christy decided to move to California and be adventurous, it was hard for me. I even wrote her a letter once that year about how much I missed her. I remember she brought the letter back on vacation to share it with me and was chuckling a little bit, mostly because it wasn't making clear sense and the writing was all jumbled thoughts. It was funny to me too. I didn't realize it was because of ADHD and the effects on my attention span that I had trouble focusing to put my thought clearly on paper.

Ironically, after all these years, toward the beginning of 2007, I was the one who moved to California. And I always go back home twice a year for Christmas and once in the summertime to my family and to my roots. That 10-year-old still lives inside of me; the one who always misses his brothers and sisters. Their well-being and happiness are never far from my mind and heart. I have never let go of them and have always been overly protective of all of them. I'm learning to do things for myself and for my happiness while simultaneously learning to trust God that they will be OK and that He can take care of them. As I am getting older and experiencing more of life, friends and traveling the world more, laughter and joy have entered my life.

For years, I had fun watching my brother, David excel in the 3 sports he was incredible at: football, basketball and baseball. In football, he was the starting quarterback back all 3 years he played and he was the star point guard in basketball. He also had the movie star looks to go with that athletic ability. David was fun to watch in basketball because he was an explosive dribbler and mover and could shoot from the outside or dribble up and do creative moves around the basket. It looked like nobody could stop him and he could just run right by his competition. In baseball, he played short stop, pitcher and was a tremendous switch hitter. One time, David hit a ball so hard at the second baseman it hit him in the neck and the guy was out. Fortunately, the guy recovered from the crushing hit. David was bold and confident in sports. He was a leader just like David in the Bible. He let his results do the talking and wasn't braggadocios and, believe me, they talked for him.

In my freshman year and David's junior year of high school, we followed a freshman bus going to an away football game against Galesburg High School. When we got off the bus, I saw that there was an ambulance on the field and somehow I knew it was David. He was the quarterback and sure enough it was my brother. The team had keyed in on getting to him and piled on him after a tackle. My brother had his leg laying behind his back and had his hip dislocated. That injury put David in a wheelchair for several months and effectively ended his football career. He eventually recovered and focused on his strongest sport—baseball. He ended up playing division 1 and semi-pro baseball, not quite making it to the big leagues.

David was always a good brother to me and made me a part of his life since I was very little. When I was maybe 3 or 4 years old, I remember he always used to say, when he was with his buddies,

"We are going to a place where tigers, lions, and bears are and I don't think you can come with us." I would always bug him and, with just a little push, he'd always let me tag along. David treated me the same way years later when David became friends with Schmitty. David, Michael and I would all hang out at Schmitty's house. We had fun there. And because he had movie channels like HBO, we watched a lot of movies at his house. We hardly ever had junk food at our house, but Schmitty did. My favorite thing in the early years at his house was stealing Oreo cookies without him catching me. Usually, he would grab me and we would get in a wrestling match. He would always kill me because he was on the wrestling team. We would be laughing our heads off during these battles.

A year later, my brother, Stevie got a bull terrier puppy. My mom said he was so ugly he was cute. I agreed, but all of us thought this puppy looked like a little baby pig more than anything else. So Stevie decided to name him Arnold after the pig that was on the TV show, Green Acres. That little dog became a part of our crew. As our friendship grew, Arnold grew up right with us. We did all kinds of crazy things with that dog. Arnold's personality reminded me of Schmitty. He was hyper and wild. They both had good-sized noses too, so they looked alike in a way.

I remember Arnold wasn't much afraid of anything. He would chew up almost anything, including white-out and shaving razor blades. He had one fear though, and it thoroughly terrified him. That was the vacuum cleaner. Whenever it was turned on, he would bolt out of the room and go hide, shivering in the bathroom. I'm pretty sure that the vacuum cleaner caught his tail once or twice and that's why he was so scared.

We used to let him chase bottle rockets. When they landed, he would bite the ones he could catch and several times they blew up in his mouth. It didn't seem to faze him at all. Bull terriers are medium-sized dogs but extremely strong. They are a smaller version of a pit bull... We had these three-foot-high bushes and we would make squeaking sounds at the other side of the bush while hiding from Arnold. From a standing position, he would hop high above the bush and land right in the middle of the bush so he could see what was making that noise. Another thing about this dog was that it really loved my mom. He would follow her around the house and stay with her in the kitchen, often sitting on her feet.

I ended up playing number one for the team and got to play a lot of really good matches. I won a lot of matches but lost to some really good players too. There were a lot of good players in our area and I remember losing to top players like Mike Kieweit and Dave Novak, among others. These were nationally ranked players that were way better than me. The tournaments were also tougher in the 16's, but I was better too. I played tournaments in Grand Rapids and ran into tough competition. I noticed I was consistent and fit, but some of these good kids were consistent and ripping the ball. I felt they were ahead of me technically.

There were so many good players like David Emdin, Jim Knapp, Greg Winchester, and my friend, Mike Kiley. All these guys were from Grand Rapids. I had lost to most of these guys in the 14's. I also played tournaments on the east side of the state and ran into some incredible players over there. I remember I did well at this tournament called Deerfield Open and two or three times I lost to the same kid, Tom Brazvich, each time in 3 sets marathon matches.

Definitely, the best player I played from that area of the state was a fantastic player named Steve Herdoiza. (Later in his college career at Northwestern, Herdo, as we called him, became a division I all-American.) I actually gave him a decent match; it was something like 6-3, 6-3. I knew I had to have challenged him a bit because he was getting really aggravated during that match. One thing I prided myself in was that even if I didn't have a great chance of winning, I was going to give a hundred percent for every ball, win or lose. I knew it was the best barometer to see where my game was at and would give me the best feedback on what I would need to improve.

I would go on showing a strong presence at tournaments in the Midwest in the 16's. In my first and second year in the 16's qualifier tournament, I started winning two, maybe three rounds and I'd have some pretty good wins, but I didn't qualify for Indianapolis. In my second year in 16's, after having a marathon 3 set win over Greg Winchester, I lost easily to a strong lefty serve and volley player named Rich Applegate. I noticed that my training on fitness had me running in circles around most of my competition when it came to foot speed. But looking back, I had no weapons and had no idea how to rip shots or take the ball on the rise. I was working like Spartan, but only getting so far and not getting the big breakthroughs I was looking for.

All I knew how to do was work harder and do whatever my coach said while searching for new ways to improve. I did become very consistent on every shot, strong strategically and became very solid at the net. Les kept pushing me to increase how many I could hit in the wall circle in a row. And by my second year in the 16 and under, I was getting over 200 in a row without missing one shot on ground strokes and volleys. I kept with Les's consistency system on the serve also and began to get higher scores on the serving test. The highest score for that test was a perfect score of 80pts and I was starting to get in the mid to upper 60's.

I became this indefatigable scrapper who could play high percentage tennis and hardly ever miss. I also would come to the net on any short ball because Les taught all-court tennis and I liked it up there. He would say that the only real attacking shots were volleys and overheads from a positional standpoint. And that was a very good thing if you were able to hit those in a match. Beside tournaments, I began to have strong results in high school tennis. My sophomore year, I rose to become the top player in my high school conference. These high school matches, along with tournament play, gave me the much-needed experience and got me used to playing high-pressure matches. I liked playing and executing strategy and grinding out tough matches. I won a lot of close matches against good players and lost some close matches too. I'd like to think that I was a courageous and fearless player. I did believe I had a fighter's chance to beat anybody. That's exactly how I played every match; I played to win.

Tennis matches were a lot like life. Growing up in our house, I learned how to strategize and make good decisions that could bring peace and love into a sometimes tumultuous environment. At our house, I saw it as a high stakes game where a kind word and willingness to help could help someone you love get through a tough time. This was pressure that helped loved ones get hope and navigate their lives. Wisdom was needed here. This game and the pressure that came with it was so much more important than a tennis match. I was used to pressure. I was a person who embraced pressure.

I liked learning to manage and deal with the pressure. The great Billie Jean King was quoted as saying, "Pressure is a privilege," and I think I saw it that way too. Slowly, at least in high school tennis, I became one of the players to beat. In my sophomore, junior & senior years, I won the regional tournament, qualifying for the state tournament each year. I went all the way to the quarterfinals in my sophomore and senior years. I was putting so much pressure on myself to succeed that I was out of balance and not mentally healthy for some time. I talked to my parents that I had started to get depressed and overwhelmed. They decided to send me to a psychiatrist and it ended up helping me a lot. I started doing this my junior year. The psychiatrist actually had me on this program where I would write down during my matches how I was dealing with things emotionally. It was like a checklist. Some of my friends and my opponents thought I was crazy, but I was so desperate to get myself together to go to play well again that I did it anyway. Looking back, I think I had obsessive compulsive tendencies. Maybe it stemmed from me trying to get through the hard times in a tension-filled house growing up. It was just my way of coping and surviving.

During high school, there was still some tough times in the house, but it was different. I had a sister who I won't name, but for quite a few years she had depression from low self-esteem. Just a supposed wrong look from a stranger or if she felt someone was disrespectful to her really affected her. She would talk about those things with me. Again, I didn't feel like a teenager; I felt much older when I got into this mode of conversation. Along with that, she had trouble finding out what she wanted to do with her life. Like I always did with my mom, I spent time trying to encourage her and listen to what she was going through.

There was a time she really upset my dad and he lost his temper and yelled at my sister. I knew she must have said something about my mom. That's the only time my dad would get that mad. That was the only time ever this type of thing with my dad ever happened and I think it was a cry for attention and help from my sister. My sister was so down that I took her out of the house and we just went for a drive. As we were talking, she said she didn't want to go back to the house and said we should go check at the Gospel Mission to see if she could get a place to stay for the night. The Gospel Mission was a place where homeless people stay. I didn't want her to stay there. Seeing her this low hurt my heart.

It was late at night and I took her there, but there were no empty rooms at the Gospel Mission that night. So instead, we went to my sister's house and we just talked on her porch. I remember the moon was full that night and so was our conversation. I listened to her talk for a couple of hours, whatever it took to get whatever was hurting her out of her heart. She always felt comfortable talking to me since I was little. I was only 16 at the time, but I was already a seasoned veteran at listening to others' problems and giving love and words of encouragement. By us working together I was able to get my sister through that storm.

Yes, like every family, there are tough times and adversity, but I had fun being in such a big family watching all my brothers and sisters grow up. I had a lot of people to look up to. There were several times where we could have had tragedy, but I believe God protected us. Four of my sisters (Bobbie, Christy, Gale & Marsha) once got in a very dangerous accident with a semi-truck on an icy road. Their car got smashed really bad, but nobody had super serious injuries, although Bobbie broke her nose on the steering wheel. Their injury could've been worse or somebody could've died that day.

Another time, my brother accidentally hit me in the back of the head with a baseball bat. It was a metal bat and I still remember the gonging sound when the bat hit my head. I grabbed my head and it was a total accident. It hurt like crazy. For some reason, Robbie started laughing, but I knew he was in shock. I knew he was terrified of what happened and was scared of how bad I may have been hurt. Besides that incident, I had had so many concussions before that. God must have been protecting me.

It was good I had my tennis to throw my passion and energy into; it helped balance the ups and downs of family life. That spring, after working so hard to get ready for the qualifier, I had my heart set on finally breaking through and qualifying for the Indianapolis sectionals. I was now in my first year in 18 and under competition. In the round of 16, I ended up playing my old friend, Jack Wallner and I now was favored to win.

Earlier that year in high school tennis, I had already beat the number one player, Jim Arvidson who was number one above Jack on Gull Lake. Later on that season, Jim did beat me in the next match, but both matches were close. After a hard fought match, I lost to Jack in straight sets and was really bummed. I had worked so hard and hadn't achieved my goal. Jack was ripping his shots, especially his forehand and I lost a close match 6-3, 7-5. I had one more chance in the back draw but had to play my nemesis from Lansing, Jason Given. I lost that match too. Jack was my friend and knew how hard I had worked. I think he almost felt bad for beating me.

I remember after losing in the qualifier, one of my peers at the club knew how hard I had worked to qualify and made a joke about my failure to make it to Indy. For that bone-headed statement, I fired a couple of tennis balls at his head, as if to say, "Screw you, I'm going to make it next year." The next year, I had one good piece of advice from maybe the best player in our area, Mike Kieweit. He said you got to quit hitting all these moon balls and you got to rip some shots and hit through the court more. I began to practice doing that more and it made a huge difference. I ended up winning my regional tennis tournament for high school again and had a really close match in the final against a big power hitter.

It was a very close match, but I was tough under pressure, super fit, and wasn't missing. I was still meeting with the psychiatrist and he told me to continue to track my thoughts to help keep them on a positive energy level. Doing this on change-overs began to annoy my opponent, but I was on a mission and I won the match. I went to state again and made it to the quarterfinals. I remember in the round of 16 I played a guy named David Emdin, who I had lost to several times and I was very nervous. David could tell I was nervous, as he even hinted at it. This time, though, I got a breakthrough and I beat David this time in straight sets. The match was close, but I was a different player. In the quarterfinals, I lost to a really tough player from Saline, Michigan. I was close getting to the semifinals but lost 7-5, 6-4. Dang! It would've been great to get to the semi-finals or win the state championships, but it was not to be.

Turns out I was prophetic because not only did I play the Qualifier Tournament and qualify the next year for the Indianapolis sectional tournament, I took a set off top seed, Todd Martin (future world #4) in the qualifying round and beat Jason Given in the back draw qualifying round with my dad watching and ended up winning the back draw. After many years of hard work and toil, I remember the exhilarating feeling of finally breaking through after beating Jason... The match was a nail-biter, which went to 7-5 in the 3rd set. I totally had embraced the pressure of the moment. I remember going up to my dad and saying, "I did it. I did it, Dad!!!!" By the way, I also beat the kid at the qualifier who had made fun of me the year before for not making it. At Indianapolis, on my first time there, I played 5 matches and won 3 rounds. I was only 3 rounds from qualifying for the national tournament in Kalamazoo. Man, the power of a dream. It was worth all the hard work.

Wisdom Nuggets

29) Believe in yourself and maximize your opportunities. One thing I had in my mind from day one when I got into tennis, from the first match I played, was that I was there to win. In my whole life as a player, there has never been a time where I didn't try my very best and run for every ball. I mentioned earlier that there were very good players who are cocky and arrogant. My attitude and energy was different. I had passion and believed I had a chance to beat anyone no matter who they were. I believe people had to really beat me and I wasn't ever going to lay down and give them the match.

30) Be the greatest you can be. Coach John Wooden, who is regarded by many as the greatest coach in basketball ever, said, "The most successful player he ever had wasn't Bill Walton or Kareem Abdul Jabaar." He said it was a lesser known player who worked his hardest and completely maximized his capabilities to the very best of his abilities. This player gave Coach Wooden his very best at all times and worked harder than everybody else. He completely maximized his potential to the best of his abilities. My whole life, I endeavored

to be that person, to give my very best and give it all on the tennis court and in the classroom. If you do that, whether you win or lose, you will stand out above 99% of people out there. In that sense, you are always the winner. It took me 7 years to do it, but I finally got my breakthrough and qualified for the sectional tournament in Indianapolis after much toil. I took a lot of lumps to get there.

Chapter 16

Goodbye Daddy Hello Father

My summer was extremely exciting and I got to play several other big tournaments. After playing the Western Closed in Indianapolis, which was my biggest goal of the last 5 years, I also played again in the Western Open at Ball State University. For this tournament, you do not have to qualify for, but I was really excited to play there. I remember we all got to stay in the dorms, kind of like college before college. All the best players in our section were there, including people like Todd Martin, Steve Herdoiza, Mark Agah, Mike Herb & Todd Occumy. I remember one match between Todd Martin and Mark Agah and it was an all-out war. Herdo and Mike Herb were cheering on Mark because they were all from Detroit area. They really were on Todd's case verbally, spurring Mark to beat Todd. It ended 7-6 in the 3rd set and Mark actually beat Todd that day. Phenomenal match.

I ended up doing very well at the tournament, getting to the round of 16 where I lost to a very good player named Jerome Mentor. The match ended 6-3, 6-3. The round before, I played a match that ended 7-6 in the third set against a guy who was top 30 in our section and I won... It was a very good win for me and he even had a match point against me. At that point in my matches, I had been doing visualization before my match. This helped keep me calm because it was as if I had already played the match. I would visualize specific strategies before the match and it helped me lock into the strategy I was trying to implement.

In this match, I was very calm even when he had a match point against me and he was about 10 feet away from me when I was at the net hitting the match point shot with his forehand. Even with him so dangerously close to me, I wasn't afraid; I just remembered what Coach Les told me to always do, which was: read the ball coming off his racket so you can see where it's going. I stood my ground and I don't know... I guess he choked and missed the sitter right in the net. Most people would just get the heck out of the way, but that's not what Les taught me to do. I just stuck to my game plan and hardly missed any shots. I remember I was coming to the net on every shot I could to his one-handed backhand and picking on his weakness because he had a humongous forehand.

Against Jerome, he didn't really have as much of a weakness to pick on. In fact, he ripped balls from both sides and had a big serve and good volleys. Every point was a battle, but eventually I felt like I got overpowered, especially on the ground strokes. At that point, my game was based on all Court play, accuracy and strategy. Later on, I'd find out you needed to develop weapons, but we didn't have that kind of technology at the club I grew up at. Looking back, I can honestly say that with the tools I was given, I maximized my results as much as I could. At the end of that year, I ended up getting ranked 59th in the Midwest. I thought I'd be ranked higher considering some of the wins I had and I knew I was better than 59th. That summer, of course, I ended up going back to the Kalamazoo Nationals and all of the top ranked national players in my age group were playing there. Watching these phenomenal players really inspired me to want to do my very best in my first year of college tennis.

That fall, I was expecting to go to Western Michigan University to play tennis, but it turned out I didn't make it because my SAT was so low that I missed it by half a point, which was required in order to play that first year. I would've had to redshirt my first year. Instead of waiting for a year, my parents and I decided to go to a different College, which was Ferris State University where I could play tennis my first year. I remember driving up to Ferris State with my mom and dad and walking on the university campus. I was going to miss my parents and the familiarity of being in Kalamazoo. They walked me around campus and later on we had dinner before they left. Thinking back, it must have been hard for both of them to have me, the youngest and the baby of the family, out of the house. They had 12 kids and now after all those years of raising us, it was just mom and dad at the house. In some ways, of course, I could see they had their freedom. But in other ways, I could see that they were sad.

Also, my dad's health wasn't good, so thinking about that kind of thing makes me sad.

Once I started going to Ferris, I stayed at a dorm called Henderson Hall and I began to enjoy the University. I remember they said something I didn't like during orientation into the university; they said that a lot of people here won't make it past the first semester at the University and they said that Ferris wasn't as strong as some other universities. I don't think that was a very inspiring thing to say to students who wanted to go there.

I had a good roommate named Ted. The only problem with him was that he was an Ohio State fan and I was a Michigan fan. We joked about that often. Next door to me, there was a guy named Kip Rustenholtz who was from Portage, Michigan close to where I'm from. Kip was funny and was a phenomenal athlete and was very good at any sports he tried. He could dunk a basketball and he was only 5 '9... I was looking forward to this tennis season and wondered what the tennis team was like. I heard they were good and, boy, that was an understatement. Man, we had a stacked team at Ferris State.

At number one, we had Agah Samarno who had wins over Andre Agassi and other top players. He also played Davis Cup for Thailand. At number two, we had Karl Johnson; at number three, we had Scott Smith who I actually think was the best player on the team, but he ended up climbing to the top 400 in the world. Number four was Kurt Hammerschmidt, number five was Mark Karrick, and number six was Matt Stanley. Mark and Scott were actually brought in mid-year. We also had another guy, Rich Applegate, who was on the team but stopped playing mid-year.

Paul Markum and I were fighting for the sixth spot because Kurt had hurt his shoulder and then they brought in Mark and Scott and didn't even let us play them. I didn't think that was fair at all. Even though I knew they were probably a bit better than us, we at least deserved a shot at it, but that is not how it went. I continued in my routine of weightlifting, speed, and agility training. In the morning at 5:30 am, I regularly got up and worked on my speed and agility. Then I would go practice with the team in the afternoon. I loved it.

There were two coaches both with the name, Scott. The head coach, Scott Schultz later climbed to one of the top positions in the

USTA organization. The assistant coach, Scott Frew, was helping run the qualifier when I played it earlier that summer before I went to college. That's where I first met him when I finally qualified for Indianapolis that same summer. The practices were fun and there were a lot of good players who usually made the starting lineup but were getting edged out because of the high level of competition. There was a really nice guy; a lanky guy named Doug Spencer and he usually made the starting lineup, but now he wasn't starting and I know that was hard on Doug. There were also other good players like Mike Friedman who I was very good friends with and played some tournaments with him. Mike had a wild roundhouse serve with not much power, but he was extremely good with the ground strokes and very good and crafty at the net. Coach Schultz wasn't really giving him a chance, but he could've been a great addition to the team. Mike had done very well at a junior college before he came to Ferris State.

    I really liked Ferris State University. People partied hard there and there really wasn't much there except the college. There was a river by the campus and we had a big tennis party there. You could go tubing down the river, which I did. It was fun. There were a lot of Michiganders there from the upper part of Michigan, which is known as the UP or Upper Peninsula. That part of Michigan is like its own nation and the people are different there. They love to hunt and, boy, they like to drink too. I wasn't a big drinker, but I could see that they could drink people under the table. I met and hung out with some great people from the UP. There were a lot of fraternities on campus and I almost joined the Sig EP Greek fraternity. It seemed like it could have been a good brotherhood for me, but I ended up not doing it.

    The girls' team was extremely good too and had won the league championship several times. They also had foreign players on the team to help boost the team's level. With both a strong girl and guy team, there was a strong spirit of excellence about the tennis programs at Ferris State. I felt like I was at the perfect school to play tennis that year because it was so challenging. There was a workout area connected to the tennis center and I used that regularly. I was closer to Coach Frew as far as working on my game technically was concerned. He helped me with my serve for quite some time and tried to get me to transfer my weight to my front foot in order to get my weight more into the court. This added power to my serve. Coach Frew also taught me how to do the split step before I volleyed to make me more balanced up at the net. Surprisingly, I'd never been taught that. There were a lot of great lessons I learned about the game of tennis at Ferris.

Later on that year, an opportunity to get a room down the hall opened up for me. I ended up not getting that room but instead got placed in a room with a guy named Larry Hart. Larry had had reconstructive surgery from getting hit by a car while on his bike. As a result, his face was not what it used to be. Within the first night, although Larry seemed like a nice guy, I knew I was in for a rough time because I had never in my life heard anyone snore as loud as this guy. I swear, the bed and the room would shake and it would get progressively louder after every snore. As he would snore, I would kick his bed to get him to stop and he would stop only briefly. But soon, the malicious assault of his snoring would begin again.

Within the first week, I got ear plugs. My first thought was to get a big rubber mallet and knock myself out with it to get some sleep, but I ended up not going that route. I started hearing comments from others close to our room how loud it was. One morning, as I was heading out of the door, I looked down and saw that someone had slid a note under our door. As I read it, I started laughing. It said and I quote "IF YOU SNORE ONE MORE TIME, WE ARE GOING TO KILL YOU!!!!!" I knew they were joking, but man was that funny.

A little over a month into my stay with Larry, two knucklehead guys who lived next door came by to say hello for a minute or so I thought. They started messing around making jokes about Larry and then got so riled up and started grabbing his mattress, shaking it up and down and trying to toss it out of the window. I warned them to stop or I was going to tell the RA (Resident Advisor). They were just laughing their butts off and somehow they almost locked me in my bathroom. Finally, I had had enough and I yelled, "LET GO OF THE BED AND GET THE HELL OUT OF MY ROOM NOW!!!" Right then and there, they quit and pulled the bed back inside the room from the window and got out of my room quickly.

They didn't know it yet, but their fate was about to be sealed. The next morning, the RA was at my door and asked when I could talk about the incident. I talked to him right there and told him everything. I knew those guys were going to be in huge trouble, but they brought this on themselves. I warned them to stop. Larry, who had been away visiting family, came back that Sunday. After hearing what had happened, he was hurt and upset. He asked me why I had allowed it and I said I didn't and that I had stood up for him and told the RA what they had done. I don't think Larry thought I had it in me to stand up for him. But when he found out I did, I could see a little smile form on his face, which showed it meant a lot to him.

The very next day I found out that the two guys who messed with Larry's bed were getting kicked out of the dorm. They asked me why I told on them and, again, I reiterated, "I told you I would if you didn't stop." There was nothing more they could say. They knew they crossed the line. Within two weeks, I was able to move out of Henderson Hall over to the tallest dorm on campus—Henry Hall. My close tennis buddies, Chris Wall and Mike Friedman, were over there and I needed a change. I also needed some sleep. I wished Larry well, but this was a great move for me. Mike and Chris were great guys and we did everything together, including studying, tennis, and going to the local bar to find girls. Mike, like me, had a learning disability and really struggled with school. I think he may have had dyslexia. Needless to say, Chris helped both of us with many of our assignments if we needed help. I won't forget one time I had to write this huge paper and it got so big I didn't know how to simplify and shorten it. Chris was so organized that he easily helped me put the paper together properly. I was already so overwhelmed that it was a huge relief to me to get such great help from him.

We started challenge matches at Ferris later in the fall and I felt really good about how I was playing. I played Paul Markham or Pauly as we called him. We had a really good match, but I won in three sets 6-3 in the third set. He was a nice guy and very competitive. Like me, he didn't take losses that well. I got to play a lot of other players that were on the lower end of the team, like Doug and they were tough matches, but I won them all. I never got to play matches against the top five players.

I continued to work very hard and set my goals to keep improving. Pauly and I played another time and he barely beat me in another three-set match. I liked the competition and I was willing to work harder to get to where I wanted. It was beginning to snow and I decided I was going to work even harder. So I decided to run on the football field with about 2 feet of snow and used the snow as resistance. I was even hitting with somebody on the outdoor courts when it was snowing and Coach Schultz saw me doing it and he was kind of blown away by that. I just was trying to reach my goals. I could tell he liked the work ethic I had. Every day, no matter what was going on, I felt like I was on the ascension because I could work harder and improve every day.

One day in December, during practice at the indoor facility, I looked up and saw my brother and his best friend, Brian Schmitt looking down at me. I knew something was wrong; very wrong. My brother motioned for me to come up and I walked up the stairs to meet him. My worst fears were realized. My dad just died of a heart attack. I was only 18 at the time and I broke down sobbing. I would not be the same after that day at Ferris. After my dad's funeral, I came back & still ended up playing Pauly for the sixth spot on the team, but lost in three sets. I fought hard but my heart wasn't there anymore. It was a miracle I even played that match. I was offered the 7th man on the team or redshirt the year, but I chose to redshirt the year instead of potentially waste a year playing a match here or there as a seventh man.

During Christmas Break, I decided to play a sectional junior tournament in Indianapolis, Indiana and stayed with a family friend from our area named Sue Foltz. My mom agreed to it and I drove out there by myself. Sue was so gracious and sweet and looked out for me. She was my guardian angel that week. I don't know where I got the strength to compete after losing my dad, but surprisingly, I felt fine. I did great in the tournament and even got to the quarterfinals. I think I did this just to prove I was going to be ok. It wasn't until one July night, many months later, while I was driving on the back roads out to our cottage, that I finally broke down due to the death of my dad. Out of nowhere, I started crying uncontrollably and kept screaming over and over, "I WANT TO LIVE!!!!!" I finally got home and burst through the front door still sobbing. My mom was right there to grab me and embrace me. She said to others there that I had finally broken down. I finished the year at Ferris and knew I wouldn't be coming back.

That summer, I was searching a lot. I was going to the Catholic Church, St. Mary's, where we worshipped while growing up. I would go and just sit on the altar when no one but God and I were there. I needed God more than ever now... My earthly father was gone now. I don't remember hearing God even speak to me on my visits to the church, but I talked to him as best as I could. I felt peaceful, especially when I was on the altar.

Looking back, I think I was putting my whole heart and my whole being in his hands because I was in need of healing. I was in need of love from my God. I always believed wholeheartedly that he was real. I never questioned it and my parents both prayed for us and taught us to pray every day before we went to bed. It was one Our Father prayer (The Sinners' Prayer) and one Hail Mary prayer every night. This time, I needed more. What I didn't realize was that not long after my prayers in that Catholic Church, God was going to want more of me.

I ended up taking a year off of college to work on my tennis game in The Detroit, Southfield area. I moved in with Aunt Jean and Uncle Bob Page. They were really looking out for me. Uncle Bob helped me get a part time job at Franklin Racquet Club, a very large and prosperous 20-court indoor facility in Southfield, Michigan. I was very fortunate to work with some great talented players and coaches. One of my coaches was Ed Nagle. He was the number one player for Michigan a few years before and he really helped me on movement and shot selection. I ended up also working with a guy named Hal Jolley. He was ranked as high as 350 in the world and helped me with my serve and volley game.

There were so many great people I practiced with and learned from at Franklin Racquet Club. Lou Graves, who was at least in his 70s, was a gentle soul and one of the 3 African American pros that worked there. Other fantastic pros were Steve Kirchbaum, who worked with the juniors and Phil Norville, who was an incredible player, especially with his volleys. Kirsh, as we called him, was a phenomenal coach and the kids loved him. He was always smiling.

Later that year, I ended up moving from Aunt Jean and Uncle Bob's place in Rochester, MI down to Southfield, MI with my cousin, Ron Page and his family. There, I was much closer to work; may be less than 15 minutes from the club. His wife, Dawn and the kids - Nathan, Kristen, Emily and the youngest at the time, Mandy, took me in like family. There were times I got lonely because I was only 19 and I was working in an adult world. Technically, I was an adult but everyone was a lot older than me. In the winter of 1988, I received a letter from Shawn, my brother's future wife. She was concerned about me and was encouraging me to get back into college by next fall. There was a lot of love in that letter and in my heart I knew she was right.

One night, I remember distinctly that I was particularly lonely and the house was quiet because it was late and I heard a very quiet and peaceful voice encourage me. It wasn't human and I couldn't see anything or anyone, but the voice told me I could do it and to keep going. The voice said it several times. And although it wasn't audible, I heard it clearly. There was a presence in the room with me. I could feel it. It made me feel like I was loved and not alone. I had never heard this voice before ever, but I knew for sure and in my mind that it was God himself. I knew it and I actually said to myself out loud that I had just heard God.

I was excited about it at the time. Later that summer, my brother, Tommy came to visit from Alaska and he asked me if he could talk to me privately. We were at our house on Woodlea Dr before we sold it in the boys' bedroom. He asked me if I knew if I was going to heaven or not. I said I thought so. I believed in God my whole life and always felt a sincere connection with him. Then he showed me in the Bible where it said, "Unless you become born again, confess that you are a sinner and ask Jesus in your heart for forgiveness of your sins you shall not enter into the kingdom of God."

I said, "I had never heard of being born again." But because it's in the Bible and I didn't want to take any chances of going to hell, I said, "Let's do this right now." So we did and that day at the age of 19, I officially made Jesus the lord and savior of my life. Looking back, I realize that God had his way of timing His entrance into my life. My earthly dad had passed into the afterlife and a little over a year later, my Heavenly Father, the God of the universe, made His entry into my life. I played and coached a whole year at Franklin Racquet Club and finally that summer, when I visited home, I decided it was time to go back to school.

Wisdom Nuggets

31) Be coachable and work hard. I had new coaches at Ferris State University and because I was hungry, the coaches would work extra with me whenever they had time. I was very coachable and would always do lots of extra roadwork and no one had ever asked me to do it. Being coachable and humble will always bring you favor in life and open doors like nothing else could. Looking back, I realized that people are always watching you, so it's very important how you carry yourself. People want to help hard workers with a good attitude. If you endeavor to be that way, you will draw blessings from all directions.

32) Lean on God first and then family during times of loss. When my dad died, my heart was broken but not without hope. My parents instilled in me that God was real and that He loved me. I believed them because I saw how much they loved me. I saw God in them, the real love of God. I saw it in their eyes and in their actions every day. The Bible says in Matthew 18:3: "You can't enter the kingdom of God unless you come to him like a child." Somehow, I had that child-like belief and faith that I knew my father's death was only temporary and eventually, I would be with him forever. I stood on that during this great time of loss and it was a rock for me to stand on when great waves of despair were crashing all around me. If you hold on with all your heart, it will be that for you too.

Chapter 17

Western Michigan University Tennis & the Miracle Woman

I decided to go back to college, so I chose Western Michigan University, which was in my home town of Kalamazoo. I liked the head coach, Jack Vredeveldt. I liked old school and he was old school. He reminded me of my parents; someone who was trustworthy and full of integrity. I remember I went to the first day of tryouts and this included walk-ons. There seemed to be over 100 people who wanted to try out. I had no scholarship, so I had to start in a tournament that had the top 20 on the team. To make travel team, you have to be in the top 8. I was nervous, of course. But as expected, I made it to the top 8 on the travel squad without much drama.

I remember the first day of practice at Sorensen courts, which is named after Hap Sorensen, a former legendary tennis coach at WMU. I saw a few familiar faces from the Junior Circuit, including Greg Williams and Brent Michaels. It was good to see them, but I was ready and excited to get on the practice court. I had one thing in mind and that was to get on the starting lineup and work my way up from there.

I remember at that time I had a history professor who was a wonderful black gentleman named Dr. Jerol Williams. We had a very positive connection and when I started having difficulties in the class, I went to his office to get extra help. He was a very peaceful and helpful man, but very soon we also began to talk about the state of our country and where it was headed. It was at Dr. Williams' office that I first verbalized my interest and growing passion to make a difference in the world and especially in the black community. Even back then, I recognized that there was an uneven playing field educationally and economically. Black people, especially in the inner cities, seemed to have a blanket of hopelessness and despair hanging over them. And whenever I saw it on TV or a friend showed those signs, it always bothered me; it always mattered to me. I wasn't blind to the injustice I was witnessing and Dr. Williams and I began to talk about the plight of the black men and women in America. These talks became full of anecdotes of economic development, education, and inspiration for the black community. Looking back, I can see that I was thinking like a community developer, a lot like Barack Obama used to do in Chicago before he became President Obama. Even back then, I tried to uplift and inspire hope in the people I was developing a growing love and compassion for.

Our conversations were very deep and Dr. Williams could see my enthusiasm to make a difference. He loved that about me, but he would gently caution me that my ambitions could be very likely snuffed out by the black community. They would have a hard time accepting me. He said it probably wasn't going to work. I understood what he was saying technically, but I couldn't accept it at all in my heart. In my heart, I could see something I don't think he was seeing. I saw that all humans, including my black brothers and sisters, really don't care how much you know but whether you really care about them. They want to know if you really love them. My plan was simply to come with my whole heart, all my gifts and abilities and with real self-sacrificing love. I was just going to be genuine and be myself. I felt that was going to tip the scale in my favor. It had to work. After my season and hopeful conversations with Dr. Williams, there would be more adventures to come later on with my connection to the black community.

I liked WMU; classes were challenging, there were lots of beautiful girls and fun parties to go to. I never drank in high school, but I started having fun and drinking a little bit in college. I had my fun with it for a while, but never quite overdid it. I was glad that when I partied a bit and did drink, I chose to do it not because of peer pressure. I had a lot of fun with it and relaxed a little bit and wasn't so uptight. That part of it was good for me, but I never did it in a way that controlled me.

A couple of years later, I was staying at a house off of Portage road in Kalamazoo with a good friend of mine who was a very good tennis player along with some other athletes, and those guys drank like fish. That was the only time I got into trouble with alcohol. A couple of times I got sick and threw up and I realized I was starting to become like them. I remember talking to my mom about how I got sick a few times and some of the people I think might be alcoholics. I told my mom that I think it would be nice if I got out of there. Within a month, I left. Even though they were friends, I just did not want to become a regular drinker or an alcoholic. I was totally dedicated to my tennis and following the rules. I would never drink anywhere near a match or before practice, except when we have a big break on the weekend or something like that. Really, it was only to relax with my friends once in a while.

 I decided to live on Campus at one of the dorms so I could get to know people on campus. That ended up being a great decision for me. I liked to eat because I had a huge appetite, and there's always a ton of food at the dorms. I had a roommate we called Weasel. He was very funny, skinny, and a really good dancer. He was also very clean and had a really good air purifier in the room, which kept air really clean. He was a good-hearted guy and was very funny to be around. Across the hall, there was a good friend of mine, Jason, who was a redhead from the country and was a genuinely good person. Those are the two people I hung around most of the time at the dorm. We did a lot of things together and they were good energy to be around.

 Being at Western, there were always great sporting events to go to. My favorite sporting event was football at Waldo Stadium in the fall even though we weren't the greatest at the time. We had just come out of a championship season, winning the Mac conference in '88, but I had to come the next year after taking a year off college. Our basketball team was better when I was there and they were contenders and I really enjoyed watching them. We were also good at hockey and one of the best teams in our league. We had a blast going to the hockey games and watched them go at it. Going to games was one good way to get away from the pressure of school and moving up the ranks of the tennis team.

 So now that I had made the top eight of the team tryouts, I started working on the next goal of making the starting lineup. I won my first match convincingly to make the seven spot, but then I was scheduled to play Scott Kilgren, who we called squirrel. At that point, I began to put in more effort to get my confidence back because I changed my game from a baseline player who came in to the net fairly frequently to more of a serve and volleyer, where I came forward all the time. At this time, my confidence still wasn't that high because that was a big change for me. I had gone through about a year and a half of losing a lot of matches I didn't usually lose to learning this new game when I was working with Coach Hal Jolley in Detroit.

The day came for me to play Squirrel and something didn't feel right. I really wasn't that confident in my ground strokes. I played the match and it was close, but I lost in straight sets 6-3, 6-4 or something like that. I was distraught and very upset. Back in the juniors, just a couple of years ago, I had two wins over the number one player, Greg Williams and I played and beat Brent Michaels, who also was the number four player at the time. Now I wasn't even making the starting lineup and I just wasn't going to put up with that and stay there.

But for now, I had to work hard and get my confidence back with my ground strokes. If I could come back and be where I believed I could be on the team, I had some work to do. I remember we were going to a match and Les, who was the number eight player on the team, said, "Jimmy, why not just hang out with me since we aren't going to make the starting lineup this year anyway." I said to him, "I'm definitely making the team this year. What are you talking about?" As the number seven player, I got to play some doubles matches and was winning those doubles matches. All these matches were pre-season matches against very good teams and a lot of the Big Ten teams.

There was a time we were going to play a certain match and I was expecting to play doubles when Coach Vredeveldt told me that I was not going to play doubles until I make the starting lineup, so I didn't get to play at this particular match. I didn't like that. It turned out that I was going to get another chance to play Squirrel and this time, I was ready and focused. Before this next match with Squirrel, I had already played Karl Davies, who we called Los and I lost that match too. I had really lost confidence in my game. I decided I had to train a lot harder and get my consistency back with the ground strokes technique I was more familiar with. The ground strokes that

Hal Jolley had tried to teach me just didn't work for me. So I went back to my old ground strokes technique and at the same time kept with my new serve and volley game.

So we started the match and I knew I was ready. I came in on every second serve to the net and just was dominating the net. I won the first set 6-1 in like 20 minutes. The second set was a battle and I actually ended up losing 6-4. The final set was just like the first, as I crushed Squirrel 6-1 in the third. He had no chance that day. My ground strokes were much more consistent this time, which I needed because Squirrel had strong ground strokes. I was serving and volleying with great precision and accuracy. This match was a very clean performance on my part. After winning the match, I felt a surge of confidence and relief. I also felt a little bit of swagger after I won the match because it was such a convincing win. One of the players mentioned he noticed me walking with more swagger and I'm sure I was because it was a big deal to win that match. With this win, I was now in the starting rotation at number six on the team. Later that year, I would play Los and beat him, and I was up to number five on the team. My confidence was now renewed, which meant that I could go even farther up in the lineup.

That year, when I got in the starting lineup, it became very exciting because I got matched up with Brent Michaels and we did very well in doubles. We started winning the matches at third doubles against most of the Big Ten teams and had very few losses. We did so well we became athletes of the week at Western, which was a really big deal. We got interviewed and we talked about what it was like to go on a winning streak like that and everyone on the campus got to read about us. We beat teams like Iowa, Michigan, Northwestern, Illinois & Ohio State.

My favorite match was against Ohio State. We played against a very rowdy team and crowd. Ty Tucker was their number one player and he was a junior legend, especially in the younger age groups. He was fun to watch play and won his match convincingly. The people in the crowd were drinking beer and saying crap to us and our coach almost mockingly. It was probably because, although we had a few close matches, we hadn't even won a match yet. Brent, or B as we called him, and I played the last match and it was a dog fight. We lost the first set in a tiebreaker and won the second set in a tiebreaker.

The third set was seesaw too. At a point they had a sitter short forehand no more than 20 feet from me. Like I always did, I didn't back up. I stood my ground and tried to read their shot and did a short reflex volley to get an advantage on them. This time, it didn't fare so well for me and they tagged me with the missile right to my left hip. I lifted up my shirt and there was a huge welt from the ball, which had smacked my skin. It didn't seem to bother me. Brent and I became more determined to fight. This set also ended in a tiebreaker. In the tiebreaker, it came to match point for Ohio State and the same scenario happened, just like when we had a short forehand and I was at the net no more than 20 feet away.

The same guy lined up and tried to drill it through me as hard as he could. But this time, I read him and I saw it come off the strings, so I was able to block it on my strings and hit back past him. That guy was totally stunned and the ball went by him so fast he didn't even have a chance to move his racquet. I loved it because they didn't even know what hit them. Needless to say, we toughed out the rest of the tiebreaker and ended up winning the match. It was so vindicating to see the whole Ohio State team slump out of there after losing that epic match. They got what they deserved for treating us and our coach so disrespectfully.

The season became an exhilarating success. I enjoyed it immensely, especially the doubles. Before the season was over that spring, I ended up getting some very bad news. My mom would be going for heart surgery because her heart was getting worse. The prognosis was that she probably was not going to make it. I was not ready to lose my mom. I remember all of us kids gathered around mom in the elevator the day we went to Bronson hospital and my brother, Robbie, started crying. My brother, Stevie, told him to shut up and quit sobbing. Then my mom said to us, "You know, I've talked to God and I told him I don't think it's my time to go yet."

After she said that, I actually believed her and was hopeful that she was going to make it. I saw the love and determination she had in her eyes, so I believed her. I think a lot of us actually did. It turned out that she went through a grueling surgery but she made it and she wasn't expected to. We were all so excited and the doctors literally called her the miracle woman. This wasn't the first time our mother had a near-death experience. She had conquered death before and she did it again. I believe there wasn't anything my mom couldn't do if she put her heart to it... God had smiled on us that day. I know my mom survived so she could be with us. That's what kept her going.

Wisdom Nuggets

33) Listen To Your Heart. When I had that problem of drinking too much and was associating with a lot of heavy drinkers, I quickly saw the writing on the wall. When you see danger signs, believe them the first time you see them. I did and I ran. Who knows what would've happened to me if I didn't. Today, my health is very good and I am a very happy person with no addictions in my life. I cut the head of the serpent off before it bit me.

34) Vision & Faith. My mom survived her surgery because she had two things, which were deeply embedded in her heart. The first one was that she had vision and that entailed the underlying love she had for her kids. The second attribute she had was faith and that was faith in God. She didn't believe it was her time to die. That faith became a shield for her from death itself. Again, the Bible in Ephesians 6:16 states: "Above all, take the shield of faith, where with ye shall be able to extinguish all the fiery darts of the wicked." What's interesting about this part of the Bible is called the armor of God section that speaks of a spiritual battle with unseen demonic entities. There are other parts of the armor of god such as the helmet of salvation, the breastplate of righteousness, the belt of truth, and the gospel of peace. Of all these pieces of armor, the shield of faith is the most important and it is ironic that a shield could guard your heart. My mom was not only dealing with her physical heart, which was in jeopardy, but also, her spiritual heart could've been in jeopardy. I believe that my mom's spirit and her faith superseded her physical situation. She truly became the miracle woman and survived to live and love another day.

Chapter 18

She's Gone

It was the end of the season after the Mac tournament and I was in coach Vredeveldt's office. He was talking about a new guy who would be getting a scholarship that's opened up because one of our players, Brandt Wegner, had graduated. When I heard that, I said to him, "But coach, what about me? I'm gonna be working hard all summer like I always do playing in tournaments. Shouldn't I be given that scholarship?" Coach Vredeveldt listened to me and then changed his mind. He decided to let us have a playoff to see who can earn a scholarship playing two out of three matches later that summer.

I was excited and ready to get to work and have a good shot at winning the scholarship. I did work hard all summer. I played on a Davis Cup Team, an adult league at the top spot on the team and did very well. Two years ago, when I won the WMTA Qualifier back draw, I should've been on the Jr. Davis cup team, but I was not, even though I had earned the right. This was sweet justice for me and I didn't disappoint and had some good wins and some tough losses as I played against other adult teams in our section.

I remember one of my matches was played on clay against a highly touted nationally ranked player, Patrick Han. I got crushed because I did not have any idea how to play on clay. I remember I had the wrong shoes and I kept sliding out of control on the clay and couldn't get my footing right. I did get to play doubles and one more singles match on the clay and I did win one round on the clay against a player I played many times. The match was close but I won again in three sets.

After that match, fortunately, I got to play indoors, which fit my serve and volley game well. I got to play a very strong player named Mitch Stevens. He played number 5 or 6 for Ball State, which was a top 25 nationally ranked division one team. I was playing really well and was hardly missing at all, executing my strategy down to the letter. The match ended in three sets. The last set was a tiebreaker and it came to a point where I had a match point with a low overhead that was really close to the net. The shot looked easy but it's a very easy one to miss. I tried to stay calm but not calm enough. Knowing I had victory in the palm of my hands, I got a little excited and pulled the shot right down into the net. I was really frustrated that I missed that point and I ended up losing the match.

Despite the tough loss, I gave my all and learned a lot from my wins and losses. After a few more tournaments that summer, I felt like I was ready for my challenge match for the scholarship. I worked toward getting mentally ready and form a concrete strategy. Visualizing my patterns of play was something to help calm me down and get focused. It's a lot like playing the match in your mind before the actual match.

The day of the challenge match came and I felt like I was ready. So I got to Sorensen court early for this challenge match and got stretched out, warmed up and calmed myself down to focus on this match... Coach Vredeveldt and my opponent, Cliff Murray, who was from Texas showed up and we were ready to play. I played very well and so did Cliff in the first set. I lost a close first score of 6-4. I thought I was playing well and felt like if I kept up with my pattern of play I was going to win the match.

I hit my stride in the second set and started to dominate the match, winning the second set by six games to one. I could see that this was really starting to get to Cliff. In the third set, I was 3-0 in no time, breaking his serve once to go up 3-0. All of a sudden he came to the net and told Coach that he was done...that he was not going to finish the match. I felt like I had broken his spirit and, instead of finishing the match, he just decided to bag it and quit.

This was only the first of two out of three matches, so I had not won the scholarship yet. We were due to play another match in about a week. I was getting ready to come and play the second match and I get a call from coach V that Cliff can't make it because his grandmother is sick. When Cliff forfeited this match, he handed me a $5000.00 scholarship covering room board and tuition. I was shocked he didn't play the match, but I sense he didn't want to have to deal with me again on the court. He just had had enough. That's my theory.

So that fall of 1990, I began my quest to move higher up on the WMU tennis team during the challenge match part of the season. My first match was against Karl Davies. Karl was a very good athlete, very fast and hits on the rise well. His serve was more of his weakness and he would kind of spin it into the court and I tried to attack it throughout the match. In this match, I served and volleyed awesome. I wasn't missing much at all with my ground strokes and was controlling the match. I won easily 6-3, 6-2.

My next match was a very important match against Brent Michaels because if I won this match then I would be getting a full ride scholarship. I was now at the #4 position on the team and if I won this I'd be ranked #3 on the team. I had my game plan ready. I knew exactly how I was going to play this match. Brent, or B as we called him, was very quick and a good topspin off of both forehand and backhand ground strokes. I knew he was going to fight hard because he didn't want to lose his position and that this wouldn't be easy. I knew, going into this match, exactly how I was going to play it.

I was able to execute exactly what I had planned and I was attacking every opportunity going to the net. I was also able to play well at the baseline and endure the long rallies that Brent could make you play. I wasn't missing at all. I was on a mission and I won convincingly 6-3, 6-3. After the match, Coach Vredeveldt came up to me and said, "Jim, that was a match without any errors." I could tell he was excited about how I had played.

The next match I would play would be against a new highly touted player from South Africa named Carl Debeer. I'd seen him play over the last year and a half and he was an explosive and very fast player with a huge topspin forehand and solid one-handed backhand. He also had gotten to the finals of the National Amateurs tournament, which is where the winner gets into the US Open qualifying tournament. Needless to say, I knew I was going to have my hands full.

The match was very tight and I was playing very well... I ended up losing 7-5, 6-3 but was very happy how I played and competed against that caliber of a player. That season, I played number three singles and number three doubles. I was really disappointed that Brent decided to play with Cliff after we had such a great season the year before. My doubles partner, Carl Davies was much better at singles than at doubles, but I just said I'd make the most out of it and help him become a better doubles player. We started out rough, but then we started to gel. I helped Carl become more strategic and play percentage tennis so we could do better in our matches. That year, after I had won the 3rd spot on the team and the scholarship, the energy was different on the team and some of it I didn't like. Cliff was talking to me and Carl Davies one day before a match at the hotel we were staying at about a traumatic experience of losing his best friend in a car accident. He said it was his fault and that he was really down. I tried to encourage him but he wouldn't listen to me. I could tell he wasn't accepting me probably because of the scholarship we competed for.

The three years I played tennis at WMU were very exciting, but there was a river of pain and rejection in the last two years. I will admit that I was eccentric and different, and people didn't always understand my thinking or actions. I simply was cut from a different mold and had been through so much I couldn't be like everyone else nor was I willing to change how I lived my life just to fit in. That wasn't me. After I won the scholarship, I was focused on continuing to move up even higher on the team. Cliff ended up playing doubles with Brent. I wanted to play with Brent or someone even better because I was extremely strong at doubles and my record proved that. I was shocked and disappointed that Brent chose to play with Cliff. Little did I know that was just the beginning of rejection from my teammates.

One day, Les, who wasn't even in the starting lineup and the only black player on the team, disrespectfully cut in front of me while at a McDonalds. He even turned around and got fairly close to me and stared me down a little bit in front of the team and coach. He was like what are you going to do about it. I wanted to smash his face, but I could have lost the scholarship, which I had spent 7 years of my life slaving away to get. Les had nothing to lose and was trying to embarrass me. I think he was just trying to fit in with all the white players instead of just being himself. Needless to say, I said, "Whatever, dude" and did nothing and kept my cool and my scholarship. Man, I was ticked off though.

Shortly after that, Cliff, out of nowhere, started getting into my face for no reason and started saying crazy stuff. Finally, I said, "What is the reason for saying all this ridiculous crap?" and got back in his face. After I said that, I turned around briefly, for maybe 20 seconds, and then Brent tapped me on the shoulder and looked at me with almost a scared look on his face and said, "YOU SHOULD NOT HAVE DONE THAT!!" I shouted back, "SOMEBODY NEEDS TO SHUT HIM UP!!!" I looked at Cliff and he looked perfectly calm. I know what probably happened; Cliff had a wicked temper and I had seen it before. When he got really mad, he would grit his teeth, narrow his eyes and look like he was going to murder somebody. I'm almost 100% sure that's exactly what happened. I know he had to be furious with me because I put him in his place in front of the team. To sum everything up, I ended up doing the noble thing, which was never getting in an altercation, staying focused on my tennis and letting people say whatever they were going to say. I refused to stoop to their level. This kind of treatment became a pattern that went on and escalated throughout the year. Cliff was the main instigator. It was a difficult time for me.

On the inside, I didn't know how to release and vent what I was going through. I wished I had gotten in an argument and yelled at some of my teammates or that one of them had tried to hit me so I could get in a good fight and get that negative energy out of me. No one ever touched me, probably because they knew I was extremely physically strong and were concerned about getting beat down themselves. Part of me wished one of them would have tried something. I would have lit them up!!! From that point on, the rest of the team began to not include me. I was so disappointed in what was going on I retreated to my own space and sat by myself many times. To get through it, I distinctly remember reading the Bible on our van rides to keep my spirits up. I was the odd man out.

The other thing with me was that I began to see and understand why people were acting the way they did. They did not want to do what was right but just fit in, even if they did wrong to fit in. It was amazing to me how most people are followers. I also was keenly aware of what God expected of me and at the time all I knew was 1) To forgive 2) Pray for those who despitefully use me. 3) Turn the other cheek. I had only been a Christian for a year. I did all three of these things.

I did all these things the Bible said to do, but it still felt bad when you are talked about and rejected. They never knew it, but I was willing to take a bunch of pain and crap for a while if eventually it might win one or all of them to Christ. To me, that was the ultimate win, much more important than the tennis or me being treated poorly. So many times I was bending over backwards listening to all this crap, but I never broke. It was like I was being crucified or something. It took all my strength at times not to take a swing at some of these guys. Because I wasn't fighting back, I believe they lost respect for me. I resisted what my flesh and anger wanted to do and it was for their benefit. Love for my enemies was at play here for real.

I learned later that turning the other cheek didn't mean you had to be a door mat for anybody. At times, I was getting so mad that I was afraid I might do something extremely violent and seriously hurt someone. I know, looking back, that keeping all that negative energy in was not good for me at all, but I didn't know any better how to handle it at the time. I was trying to do what was right and this was the only way I felt right about handling it at the time. Now I know it would be better to take someone to the side and give them a good piece of my mind to get that negative energy out of me. If they came after me physically, it would be self-defense.

Basically, not only did I not want to lose my scholarship, I also didn't want to get hurt or possibly hurt somebody. Most importantly, I cared about these people's souls and what kind of witness would I be if I lose my temper and get in a brawl? If I do that, I become the problem, even though I was minding my own business and didn't start any of this. If I react physically and start a fight, I lose.

What I do today is, I practice forgiveness and I continue to pray for these same people who, in some ways, betrayed me. To me, I'm looking at the ultimate victory, which is getting them to know Christ in spite of what happened to me. It's worth the sacrifice to me, even though I felt like I was dying inside. If I can behave in a way that can get them to know Christ, it will be totally worth the pain I went through. In the poem "IF" by Rudyard Kipling, he says, "Don't give way to hating." There have been times, even though this happened over twenty years ago, I felt resentment and tremendous hatred toward my former teammates who disrespected me. Sometimes, I had brief patches where I felt hate consumed me.

Even when this was actually happening, I struggled with the mask of pain, anger, and hatred. I had to resist that. That could have easily turned me into an evil, mean person. Mainly, it was just the residual pain that remained. I later asked God with, at times, a strong feeling of resentment, "Why did I do what you said by forgiving my teammates and also praying for them, yet my reward seems to be that I'm the one who is left hurting." Over the years, I had to look deep within myself to reason that out. These guys weren't all bad people, but I had one or two people turn against me and they influenced the majority of the team to reject and judge me.

I was never able to share who I was at my core with these people on my team and that was something that saddened me. One day, at the end of my second season, Greg, our team captain, came up to me and said, "Jimmy, I think you need to find some new friends." Wow, that was hard to hear, but he was right. I wasn't one of them. I didn't fit. I looked at myself at that moment and wanted to fit somewhere. I believed in team and I loved to win. Deep down in my soul, although they didn't want me, I wanted them to know God if they didn't already know Him and to be on the ultimate team, which was the one who knew the Lord Jesus Christ. I held that quietly in my heart even at the pinnacle of my rejection.

A part of my soul wanted to fight back and defend myself, wishing I had handled things differently. Ultimately, now I realize I may not have won the battle back then, but I know now I have won the war. I didn't let anger and hate consume me. I still walk in love and want the very best for these people after all these years. Anyone can get mad and get in a fight to defend their pride, but very few can restrain themselves and love and be the better man. I won in this situation no matter how I was treated. Truly, there is a poetry to the pain, much like a weeping willow blowing in a great storm. It bends, but it never breaks. I can say I was like that weeping willow in the storm. Although my heart was bruised and at times broken, God gave me great strength and wisdom to overcome it all. As the scripture states, "He who desires to be greatest will become a servant of all," even servant of your enemies.

Early that fall, after the challenge matches and a few pre-season matches, I got a call from my brother, Stevie telling me he had some bad news. He said that mom was sick and she wasn't going to get better. This time around, her heart was failing and there's nothing that can be done about it. I was in shock. I was used to my mom being a superwoman and she could overcome anything. I knew in my heart that this was the truth and that she wasn't going to be with us much longer.

When I came home and saw how my mom looked, she was very weak and I could tell her light was dimming more and more every day. She couldn't walk by herself without assistance. I helped her to the bathroom, assisting and almost carrying her there. We had bought her a daybed so she could sleep downstairs because she was in no condition to climb stairs... The location of the daybed was great because there was a lot of sunshine coming through the window in the morning and into the afternoon. My mom had frequent visitors who loved her. To me, they were more like angels. Mrs. Cortez would come down regularly to sit and fellowship with my mom. There was also Mrs. Mackarty and Mrs. Snyder who were over all the time. I could tell they really did not want to lose my mom just like all of us.

She was so deep in all our hearts. Every day I looked at her, she was so tired and her eyes were tired, but love never stopped flowing from them. Her love was constant. She didn't have the strength to be the mom she wanted to be, so I watched her just savor the time she had left with us. There was nothing I could do to stop this; all I could do was love my mom as much as I could while she was still here. One day, we had to bring mom to the Borgess hospital and they actually had to airlift her later that week to the Mayo Clinic. It wasn't long before they brought her back. I wondered if maybe it was possible they could do a heart transplant, but we weren't on the list for that.

Once they brought her back, we all knew she had a very short time left. There was nothing they could do for her. I saw my mom go through a lot of pain and tears at the end. I watched over her and watched everything just like I had my whole life. The doctors prepared us for what was to come. They said her heart was winding down and it was eventually going to stop beating. I watched every beat as it began to slow more and more. It came to the last day of her life and the doctors said we could go into the room and watch her take her last breath. I watched on the heart monitor every heartbeat as it slowed and I watched her face simultaneously. When I heard the last heartbeat on the monitor, I looked at my mom and her mouth and eyes were open. To me, I imagined she was seeing God at that very moment. She was gone. She was with God now.

Wisdom Nugget

35) Hope. When I saw my mom die, it was hard. Just like the death of my dad, I always had it in my heart that I would see them again. They were with Jesus and I knew and believed that. I saw how they lived their life and blessed others, so I knew they were in heaven. I'm sure I blocked out losing my parents, but I really haven't thought about them that much since they were gone. Maybe it's too painful for me to handle. What I do know, for sure, is that deep in the recesses of my heart I know I will see them again. It's that hope that has anchored me and given me peace after all these years of losing two of the dearest people of my lifetime.

36) Visualize what you want: For me, visualizing in detail how I would play my matches was powerful. I found out years later that visualizing my future and where I really wanted to be would be very key to my success in all areas of my life, be it physically, socially, spiritually, and financially. Many years ago, I wrote a poem about the desolation in the inner cities and wrote about hope and greatness coming from there. I wrote about being a big part of that renewal as much as I could. Now over 12 years later, I am walking in it in real life, making a difference every week in the lives of inner city families in the south central Los Angeles and surrounding areas. It's happening because I never let go of the vision that was in my heart.

Chapter 19

Summer in Saipan, a Summer of healing

After my mom passed, it was a very hard time. We had the funeral and the church was packed. My mom knew so many people and I felt the respect and the love from the people. Just like at my dad's funeral, my brother, Finley, sang melodiously the song Amazing Grace. There wasn't a dry eye in the whole place and it didn't hurt that he had the voice of an angel. As his voice filled the cavernous church edifice, it helped us embrace each other as a family and we shed tears; tears of love and sadness.

I sat next to my sister, Maggie and we held hands tightly almost instinctively to get through the service. We didn't let go the whole time. Reality was hitting hard and we couldn't bring her back. I knew and everyone in our family knew we had each other and that was enough. My mom's ashes were to be divided in half and buried on top of my dad's grave, while the other half was to be poured in the middle of Gull Lake. We had this huge aluminum mixing bowl that she used to make her bread in and we had her name and her life span engraved in it. We put mom's ashes in that bowl and about 6 or 7 of us rowed it into the middle of the lake.

When we got to the deepest part of the lake, we all said goodbyes to mom through tears. I'll never forget when we dropped the huge bowl with her ashes into the lake. We all watched it go down slowly and I kept watching as long as I could until I couldn't see it anymore. In my heart, I knew I wouldn't see her again in this world but we would always be connected no matter what. I already was looking forward to when I would see her again in the next life. I truly had that hope, and death had no permanence with me.

As I look back, I am thankful that I had my mom for 21 years. I really needed her as an example and pillar of strength to gleam from. If I had lost her when I was 5, I would not have experienced all the amazing attributes she had to offer. She lived her life fully and with purpose. She was an everyday constant in our lives and she did it with passion and with undying love. She gave her whole heart for us until it literally didn't beat anymore. I can't wait to see her again.

Within a few days after the funeral, I had it on my heart to speak to members of my family. I was doing what I had always done, which was look out for everyone. This was, I felt, an important and pivotal time in our family. When I got everyone together, I said, "We have to stay together. I know some here are struggling to believe that you can be happy and get what you want in life, but you can have it. You can have everything that you want to bring you fulfillment. We need to be there for each other no matter what." I think some of my family members half-heard me and others were just in another place when I said what I said. But I'm glad I got that out of my heart and shared it. It was burning in there for so many years for all of them and it felt good and liberating to let their ears hear it. I needed to release that love, and I did.

That spring, after finishing my second year of college tennis, my sister, Christy, invited me to spend summer in Saipan, a US commonwealth where she had now been put in the distinguished position as an assistant attorney general of the island. I said yes to the invitation and couldn't wait to go. I needed to get away from all things serious and just heal from the loss of my mom. I decided I would get away from tennis for once and have more fun, plus see what not being so dedicated to my sport was like. I knew I had another person in there. Christy, although she had a serious job, was a free spirit and an independent adventurer.

I knew we were going to have fun and my big sis' didn't disappoint. We went caving, sailing, traveled to other islands like Tinian, which is where the atomic bomb pits are. We went to Suicide Cliff, which is where the Japanese marched their whole families to their death in World War II to avoid being captured. There was so much history and mystery on this island. One day, my sister took me to this part of the island where there was a jungle. She said there were spirits of the people who died in World War II living in that Jungle and no Islanders would go in the jungle because they were terrified of those spirits. She said that when we go by the jungle you can actually see a haze of the spirits on the outskirts of the jungle. We went there to look at the jungle and I saw the haze. Literally, my hair stood up on my arms when I saw it. We had many unique and fun adventures like that.

I really enjoyed the simple house and life my sister lived and how we got to bond again. I was with family and she was still the same funny person but just with a lot more responsibilities. We ate food similar to what the islanders ate. There was a lot of fish, but we still had American foods like chicken, hamburgers and pasta. Stuff like that.

I ended up getting a part time job as a tennis coach and a beach activities coordinator at a resort. I don't think I ever worked for more than 15 hours a week. After work, I would go to the beach volleyball court and play for hours with mainly locals. That was unique because locals didn't usually get along with white folks, but we did get along fine. I quickly made friends with two local brothers, Glenn and Jesse. From then on we did everything together. They already had their girlfriends and soon enough I had mine too. Her name was Chizico, a beautiful vacationing girl from Japan. I got to do so many cool things with someone from a different culture. Glenn and Jesse were from the indigenous Chamorro people.

Me on Saipan Beach.

The island had been invaded several times by the Spanish and Germans and locals were not treated well. There had been relations with all these different ethnic groups, so there were people on the island with blond hair, blue eyes, and dark skin. Because of these invasions, the Chamorro had a history of hatred and distrust of white people and with good reason. Despite this history, my relationship with the small group of locals began to thrive. One of my favorite times with my new friends was when I got invited to their home up in the mountains where we cooked fish from the ocean over the fire and ate there native food. I was one of two white people invited to come and I knew I was officially welcomed into their world. They trusted me. This was a rare thing and I knew it. There were at least 15-20 other locals there at the feast. I felt very privileged indeed.

The rest of the summer was beautiful. On one adventure, my sister and I went hiking and caving with a friend and guide named Crazy Jake. He was a 50-something years old hippie-looking dude, who I was warned wasn't all there upstairs. He was famous for being a lumberjack who almost killed himself falling out of a giant tree. He was our guide.

After going through so many beautiful and also creepy caves and walking high above the ocean on some cliffs, we came to this pass. He hooked his foot on the other side of this pathway, but in between was a free fall. And if you slipped, you would fall to your death on the jagged rocks at least 50-70 feet below. He went right through it and never looked back at me. I started yelling and swearing at him, but he ignored me. If I didn't go through the pass, he would have left me and I had no way of getting home. I went through the pass against my will and fortunately didn't fall to my death... Fortunately, I escaped unscathed. That summer was a special one I will never forget. I had a great birthday party on August 18 shortly before I went home. I was feeling sad indeed. I remember a typhoon was coming when I decided to go home. I almost went to Hawaii for a week, but instead went home to finish my last year of college tennis. Mom was gone, but I was going to be ok. She really never left me. She was in my heart forever.

Wisdom Nugget

37) Healing In His Wings. God, just like the last time mom had a heart attack, opened the door for us as a family to heal by going on a trip to Colorado. This time, with my mom's passing, I needed rest and healing and I got it on the other side of the world in Saipan... God's angel, in the form of my sister, Christy, gave me an escape to get away from everything serious, including tennis and just rest, chill, and be with family. God is faithful.

Chapter 20

CLC, Rodney King, and Amway

From Saipan, I entered my last year of college tennis. I wanted to finish strong and I worked my way up to the number two on the team. I had barely lost to Carl Debeer 6-4 in the third set. I was very close to being number one on the team. I played number one doubles with Carl and we did very well once we started to gel. We won the Bowling Green Doubles Invitational, which was a really big college tennis tournament. I remember we were about to lose in the quarterfinals and I pulled Karl aside and said, "Look man, let's make a few adjustments strategically so we can come back in this match", and we did. We got all the way to the finals and won a great three-set match against Bobby Zumph and Michael Westbrook. I was so excited that I finally won a college tournament, especially at an away site. That year, I got to the finals at number two singles and lost to Brian DeVirgilio in the Mac tournament and Carl and I lost in the finals in the Mac doubles.

At this point, I also had gotten involved with some really solid Christian organizations on campus. The first one was called Inter-varsity. I loved going to that because there was a great energy there and the powerful presence of God due to the worship I experienced at those meetings. Later that year, I got involved with a Christian group called Chi Alpha and that's where I ended up staying the rest of my days in college. I met a lot of good people there and I ended up becoming roommates with some of these great guys from Chi Alpha. My roomies were Matt Slocum, John Heika, Pete Johnson, and Joseph Haddad, who was from Lebanon. Two of my close women friends were Jen Skibba and Cindy Chia, who I am still good friends with till this present day. The other Christian fraternity I became a big part of was called Alpha Omega started by my great friends Donyll Lewis and Gil Garret way back in 1991. It's predominantly a black fraternity from whom I still have life long friends till this day.

As I was getting immersed into college Christian groups, there was also, at this time, a big racial storm brewing in America. Rodney King had just got beaten down by the police and it was all on video tape. The trial was coming up that spring in April and there was high hopes in the black community that these cops would be prosecuted and brought to justice. I just moved to a different dorm called Henry Hall and there were big discussions going on in the black community at that dorm about how the trial will turn out. On April 29 of 1992, the court came with its verdict. All the cops were acquitted despite the brutality they unleashed on Rodney King that day. When I saw my black friends all gathered in mass in the Henry Hall dorm lobby, I could see the hurt and hopelessness on their faces, and I heard outrage in their dialog. It was as if they had been shot through the heart. As I heard them vent, they spoke of how the system of the government and law enforcement were intent on keeping them down and oppressed unjustly. I totally agreed with them.

As I stood there with them listening intently for about 40-45 minutes, I realized something very important. Everyone I was listening to was admitting defeat and forecasting their own hopelessness and future doom. I realized that all these wonderful and powerful black citizens were giving their power away to a system that didn't deserve one morsel of it. I could clearly see that the history of oppression since slavery still weighed on my friends' shoulders. It had been passed on to them and the court case decision on Rodney King only reinforced that pain and pressure. At that point, I knew I had to say something, I had to say something poignant and powerful right now. I spoke up and said, "I need to say something. Can I please share something?" The leader of the whole gathering stopped, signaled everyone to be quiet and said, "Let him talk."

I said, "I have been listening to everyone here speak and I totally agree with you that this court decision is a complete travesty. I keep hearing you all say how the government and the powers that be are against you and are stopping you from advancing in America and I agree. I see and believe they are. What I see happening here is that most of you believe that without government's help and the people in power you can't thrive like you want to. But that's not true. You don't need them and you are giving your power away to them!!!" Once I said that, everyone really started to believe my message. I continued, "Whatever you want here in America, you can do from within, from within your own people and also collectively with people like me who want to be a part of this movement. The white people, with their prejudice, were not born that way; it was a learned behavior. Someone in their circle poisoned them this way. It's vital you do not become hateful and ugly like the people who have oppressed you. They are the ones in the real prison of hatred and prejudice, so don't put yourself in that prison too."

We continued to talk at length. As I looked at each and every one of them looking at me while I talked, I saw that the countenance on their faces had changed. I feel that the pain had lessened in their hearts and hope and strength were rising in these beautiful Americans once again. The leader began to speak to the people and he had a smile on his face. He said, "Maybe we should have Jimmy come with us to our next NAACP meeting." Everyone wanted me to go. I said that I definitely would want to go, for sure. I was so excited about what had just transpired that day. I realized that I could make a big impact on a cause that was so important. I simply came with my whole heart that day with love, passion, and compassion and it was more than enough to make a difference. I knew it would be, and it was proven true that day.

I had a friend from church named Lafaunce. He took some time to go through the Bible with me at that time and he was also there at the Rodney King meeting with me. I was so excited and was looking forward to being a part of making a difference in this movement. So the next day, Lafaunce and I discussed my next step. He said straight out that I wasn't mature enough as a Christian to handle what I was talking about. He also said that the people were already looking up to me for leadership, but until I get a stronger relationship with God I could end up doing some things that can hurt people because I felt I could do this on my own without God's direction. I thought about what Lafaunce had said and I was really disappointed.

As I thought about it, I just said he was probably right and I pulled back from going to anymore meetings about Rodney King's trial or the NAACP. I wanted to make sure I had a better foundation in the word of God and my relationship with God and also, I didn't know if I was ready to jump into this. I was very zealous to make a difference and that kind of scared me a little bit. Although I didn't jump right into this cause like I wanted to do at the time, I never forgot what happened that day and knew that when I am ready I'll be back and use my voice for the greater good in this cause in the black community.

It was in 1993 that I was taken to a church called Christian Life Center on Portage road. This would change my life for many years to come. I remember walking through the door and hearing Pastor Joel Brooks for the first time. He was a black man with a multi-cultural church and an incredible message that day. It was bold, provocative and it was right up my alley. Pastor Brooks thought differently; he thought outside the box and I knew this would be my church home right away. I was to be at this church for 15 straight years from 1993 to 2007. I loved Pastor Brooks' messages, but I was closer to the assistant pastor, Armstrong, who did most of the counseling at the Church.

Pastor Brooks did almost all the preaching for the most part, but Armstrong was just better at counseling. It was just his gift. Don't get me wrong, when Pastor Armstrong would preach, it was fantastic and he always had a lot of bullet points you could take home with you. Five steps to success or five steps to overcome a broken heart. His messages were fantastic also. What I really appreciated about Pastor Brooks was that his messages were bold and he would say things that were true, which needed to be said but weren't always popular. I really liked having a courageous pastor. There were also many good classes I got to take at CLC, as we called it. There were classes on finances, spiritual warfare, prophetic training and many other vital areas of life. The speakers they brought in were phenomenal. Some of my favorites were Bishop Dale Bronner, Mike Murdock, Ed Cole, and Bishop Joseph Garlington.

I loved how we worshipped God at this church; the music was fantastic and Pastor Brooks was a great musician himself and was a keyboardist, formally part of the band, Junior Walker and the All-Stars, which was a very famous band. The worship wasn't a show, but instead was a genuine pursuit to commune with the living God.

Pastor Joel Brooks was a unique man who had a unique story. There was a time in his life he didn't like white people. But when he tried all the different religions, he finally settled on Christianity and God changed his heart and life. He was shown that God wants all the races to be together and that if he was going to serve God, then he would start a church that included all races. God changed his heart and, in fact, was changing the world of Kalamazoo through the vision that God had given him. As for me, my heart was into reaching souls for salvation. To me, it was simple. What could be more important than where you spend eternity? I felt that burden deeply back then and still do today. That is a true heart of an evangelist.

I was looking for trainings on evangelism at our church, but they didn't have it there. Although I loved my church, there were many times I felt like I was never going to get to use my gifts, but I served anyway. I struggled for many years, feeling like my gifts weren't being used and wondered why there was a delay with regard to me using my calling. Experiencing this pain was not what I had expected in following God. There were so many times I would get depressed and felt like I couldn't really hear God. I wondered if there was something I was doing wrong with regard to why doors didn't seem to be opening for me. I, many times, felt helpless, trapped and I had no control over my circumstance or destiny.

I remember, not long after I started going to Christian Life Center, they had a woman come and preach. Her name was Prophetess Diane Palmer. She was a beautiful singer and a psalmist and God was giving her words about people's life both past, present, and future. There was no way she could've known any of these things. I had never seen someone getting a word from God to foretell the future. She was going around the room and all of a sudden she paused and stopped at me. I could hardly believe what she said about me. When she began to speak, it was as if she had known me since I was a little kid up to my present age of 23 years old. It was as if she knew the struggles I had been going through growing up. I wondered how she also knew that I have the desire and passion to become an evangelist in the ministry and reach people for God.

I remember the exact words she said regarding my family, like it was yesterday. She said, "You didn't want to believe me because you thought I had failed you, but I've been proving myself over and over again. Don't you know it's true? So watch. You'll go back to the ones that are back there waiting for you. You'll draw them unto me because you had to see a living God and they'll have to see me too." The prophecy went on to say, "You watch, I'm going to develop you. I'm going to build evangelism inside of you, you'll preach and give prophetic words, and signs and wonders and miracles will happen. Because death was all around you, it tried to take you. But I healed and utterly delivered you. So you watch and see. 93 is over; 94 has just begun. God is going to turn the tide, son." When I heard this, I was stunned. Prophetess Palmer had just spoken the exact things in heart with regard to helping my family to know God and laid out my great ambition to make a difference in the world as an evangelist, not to mention speaking of the tough things I went through with my family as a child. There was no way she could've known all this without God telling her.

That church service with prophetess Palmer came 2-3 months after I joined CLC. I was ready for that prophecy to come to pass now. It didn't happen that way. I kept anticipating that I would step into my calling as an evangelist. Months and months went by and nothing happened. I thought it was no big deal. When years started to go by with no sign of anything opening for me, trusting God that I would ever be an evangelist became a real challenge for me. This would be a primary issue I would brood over and be frustrated about for years. I would wonder many times if God just could never use me or maybe I just wasn't good enough person that God could ever use someone like me.

After 11 years of being at Christian Life Center, I was at the end of my rope and felt I was at a dead end at this church. Part of me felt like giving up, but I couldn't. I knew something had to change and I was tired of being frustrated. Then I came across a tape series called "Molded by the Master" by Pastor Kevin Leal. I felt that God was leading me to surrender to him and give the dreams and calling he gave me back to him. I also felt him telling me that I just need to practice loving him and not worry about when those dreams would come to pass. This tape series further gave me a new revelation of another thing I needed to do.

It spoke of how God makes us into different kinds of vessels depending on your attitude towards him. There are broken vessels, vessels of dishonor, vessels of honor, and finally chosen vessels. Kevin's tape series said you can tell what kind of vessel you are becoming by how you talk and what's coming out of your mouth. In other words, out of the mouth, the heart speaks. And you're either a complainer or a positive proclaimer who lives by faith. I decided that day that God wasn't the problem; it was me and that I was going to decide to be a chosen vessel by beginning to be positive and speak life to my situations, which seemed hopeless. I decided that, although I wasn't great at hearing God at the time, I eventually would get there even if I had to crawl there by the skin of my teeth.

I also began to focus on small victories. For example, I knew that if I was reading the word of God or meditating on it, that was a form of hearing God and encouraging myself with specific scriptures. One of my favorite scriptures was, "God inhabits the praises of his people." If I verbally and physically was praising and worshiping God with my voice and my body, I knew that even if I didn't feel it in faith, he was there; he was in my presence when I did that according to the Bible. Another encouraging scripture that helped me was, "If you abide in me and my word abides in you, anything you ask will be given to you." That scripture gave me hope because it promised that the desires of my heart will come to pass if I just kept living in God's word and obeying it.

This was a very humbling process for me, but it was the first time I truly began to trust God and have peace. Basically, I began to let go of control of my life on this day. This was definitely a process, but I made a decision to do it, so it was a huge deal that I was doing this. The irony of the story was that after less than a month of releasing control of my dream to God, my dream came to me and I got to speak and do evangelistic work at two different colleges, which I had never done. Basically, I let my dreams go out of my hands and God quickly brought my dreams to come to pass in a very short time. During this time of surrender, God brought me back to all those years I seemed to be waiting around and being ignored by Christian leaders and seemingly the doors were not opening up for me for 11 years.

What God showed me was that I didn't need them to promote

me and that he had me all to himself all those years. Yes, despite how I felt and how frustrated and angry I was at Him, I couldn't see how he actually was developing me and teaching me through life's trials the whole time. The thing was, I couldn't see his handiwork until He had completed the job. I, at that time, realized that God was the biggest trip in the whole universe. He was cutting away things in me that needed to go so it would not wreck what he was going to do with me as an evangelist later. I came up with a name for this valley I seem to be in. I called it "The Land of Anonymity". I called it this because no leadership ever took notice of me or considered me as someone to invest in or promote. It's like God was hiding me. It felt like rejection to me. In this land, I saw it was a land of death and it was the death of the different parts of me.

God actually showed me images of faces in this land, which intrigued me greatly. The faces I saw were things like pride, fear, being a controlling person, hate, and even lust. In this land, everything was a color of gray and a pasty white-like death. When God showed this to me, I looked back at this land and saw these faces, which were the old me and they were frozen in grotesque facial poses like statues, but the poses were a tortured look. Any time I walked backward into the Land of Anonymity, the faces would start to come alive again and I realized I could become those faces again if I didn't resist them and stay close to God and the teachings in His word.

If I went back to being controlling, that face would revive and come alive. If I went back to regret or hating or pride, they all would come alive too. When I saw these faces, I decided it was better to run toward God because the old me was a waste land. This movie of myself and the old me showed me that what I needed to know most about God is that the pain I was going through while waiting for my calling to come to pass was really God's massive love for me. He was protecting me and the people I would reach someday from me, which would've wrecked everything and hurt a lot of people. I knew now that without trust in God I would've tried to do things on my own and none of what I did would've lasted because when you think everything is achieved because of your own power, it's all control and pride. Pride comes before the fall.

One door that opened and was introduced to me was a powerful networking business called Amway. When I got involved, I liked it more and more. I tried networking before, but once I got to the different seminars and saw the quality of people that were leading in the business, my respect grew. My dream was to become financially independent and have more time to impact people's lives in a positive way through motivation and inspiration and God's message of salvation. What I loved about Amway business was that it had a system to develop you on a daily basis with proven mentors that you are accountable to every month if you were coachable.

Me in my Amway suit and tie.

It was so good to see in seminars a new breed of people that were successful and they earned where they were at. It wasn't given to them; they had to become a better, more disciplined person to achieve their success and you could tell that when you heard them speak. I was learning things I never learned in school from the books, tapes, and seminars. I was learning how people were emotionally tied to their job and weren't being creative or being entrepreneurial anymore. I saw that in this environment, it was all about entrepreneurship and developing a new success mentality. I felt like I was given a race track to run on. I learned to cultivate a dream that I would chase and that felt so good to me. I felt I had a purpose in life and was happy I could help others envision their life and inspire them to go after their dreams too.

Basically, I couldn't be successful without helping other people achieve their dreams. I knew in my heart that was a good thing. I spent six straight years putting my heart and soul into the business and was able to have some reasonable success developing a business of over 200 people nationwide. I made some decent money and had some really good months where I made over $4500.00. But when things weren't sticking, I decided to go back to school and get another degree to give me more stability.

My new degree would be in physical education, which I finished in 2005. It was right about this time that I finally met a wonderful girl I felt had the potential to be my wife. Her name was Sarah Masters and we were together for over two years. We had so much in common. Both of us were from big families and my family loved her immediately. When she told me that her family used to have so many cars at their house and that people complained it looked like a used car lot, I just started laughing. That just warmed my soul and I was happy to hear that because her family was just like ours. One thing I loved about Sarah is that she was extremely thoughtful and giving. I really think she was at least a half angel. I called her the card queen because she always sent actual Christmas, Birthday cards, etc. to tons of people. We were not only dating, but we were best friends too.

As the relationship developed and we got closer, we began to do more of the things couples do. We started going to some of her friends' weddings and I enjoyed the first one. But then, not long after, there was a second wedding. I began to realize that Sarah had a lot of friends. Through our whole relationship, I think we went to 6 or 7 weddings. I didn't know if she was giving me a hint that she wanted to get married or not, but I think this may have been a subtle hint. I remember when I went on my first trip to go meet her parents in St. Louis. I love St. Louis, but it is really hot there in the summertime. I loved going to amusement parks; so we went to Six Flags theme park. I remember I went on a roller coaster ride right away and I got really dizzy and almost sick with motion sickness. I was about 34 years old and I couldn't believe this happened to me. We also went out walking in the Forrest, but I could not believe how hot, humid and muggy St. Louis was in the summertime. It was almost unbearable.

Sarah and I did everything together. She was very good at soccer and I went to many of her games. When I played tennis tournaments, she was always there to support me. Of course, I had dated before but had never found someone I felt I could get serious with until Sarah. I enjoyed all the seasonal and holiday things we did together. I liked being with her and holding her when we watched movies, especially romantic ones. Her favorite was The Notebook and I loved it too. I ended up going down to St. Louis three or four times with Sarah. As we got closer, we began to talk about marriage. One time, while I was driving back from St. Louis, Sarah blurted out that she wanted to have my babies. Deep inside me, I really loved that this woman wanted to have my children.

Sarah said it was a good idea if we went through a book on relationships and about people who were considering getting married, so I decided to do that with her. We went through the book and the chapters together and it was helpful. I learned a lot about her wants and needs as a woman emotionally, financially and, yes, sexually. We covered the whole gamut. We got to the part where we talked about where we were going to live and what we wanted to do and if we were compatible. I thought we are very compatible, except I wanted to travel more and be a global evangelist and that's not what Sarah wanted.

Sarah was my best friend, but I began to realize that this may not work. She wanted to be home where she was in her house in Kalamazoo, but I wanted more than that and I wanted to expand and become successful rather than just settling for where I was. I realized that although I loved Sarah, we weren't a fit for marriage. I remember the day we met at a restaurant to talk about whether we were going to stay together. I remember the words I said. I said, "I just want to be free. I need you to let me go."

It was hard for me to say those words. Sarah agreed and she seemed very calm. I knew she was just keeping her cool. But just like me, I knew it hurt her that we were going to be separated and not together anymore. As time passed, Sarah found a person that was good for her and they began to date. I knew I had to leave her alone and that we shouldn't be friends anymore. That made me sad because she was my best friend. She ended up staying with that guy. A few years later, they got married. They have a couple of kids now. I still wonder how Sarah is doing and still miss her. I know I wouldn't have been happy if I wasn't doing what I was called to do and I was married and not in the right place. I believe I made the right decision, even though it hurt.

Two years after finishing my physical education degree and maybe a year after breaking up with Sarah, something unexpected happened. I felt like God was calling me to move to California. I had met Pete Fischer, the former coach of Pete Sampras, at the Kalamazoo Tennis Nationals. After hanging out at a few of Pete's practice sessions, I asked if I could work with him in California sometime. Pete said I was more than welcome. I was very excited that I'd be learning tennis from a legendary coach. I'll never forget the first day I was to train. I was told I may be a hitting partner for the reigning US Open champion, Maria Sharapova.

We all met with Maria and her whole team of coaches at the USTA Training Center in Carson, CA. Instead of hitting with Maria, she instead hit with a very good junior player at the time, Daniel Nguyen, who after high school ended up playing number two for USC a couple of years later. Of course, I wished it was me, but it was awesome to see those two go at it. When their match was over, I briefly congratulated Maria on her tremendous victory at the US Open the previous year. I, out of respect, wanted to give her space because I'm sure people get star struck and want something from her all the time. Later on, I did get to train with US Davis Cup player and former world #18, Vincent Spadea and also with Wimbledon semifinalist, Alexandra Stevenson, the daughter of an NBA legend, Julius Erving or, Dr. J, as he is famously known. Both were fantastic experiences for me. It was at the USTA training center in Carson, CA that I realized and even had a premonition that I was going to move here.

A month later, I got invited to a tennis seminar in Irvine California with another tennis mentor of mine named Oscar Wegner. He was also a global name in Tennis. It was there that I got offered a job to teach tennis in Laguna Beach and I took the job. Initially, Nick Hernandez, a Laguna Beach tennis coach offered the job to my friend, John Carpenter, but he said he couldn't do it and pleaded that I should be talked to and recommended that I'd be a great fit. Nick and I talked and I, knowing it was a great opportunity, said yes. It was the best decision of my life. God opened a whole new world for me in California.

Wisdom Nuggets

38) Proverbs 24:6 states, "For by wise counsel, thou shalt make thy war: and in multitude of counselors there is safety." I had great counsel in two areas at this time in my life: 1) From millionaire mentors in the Amway Business, which included books, tapes and seminars that changed my thinking about life, vision and the diligence it takes to reach your highest dreams in life. 2) The other was that I had spiritual mentors that guided me in my relationship with God and I tapped into the great power, wisdom, and love he had to offer to guide every area of my life. I learned to surrender to him and truly trust him to guide my life after about 15 years. When that happened, then and only then did I have peace.

Chapter 21

California Dreaming

I first drove cross-country to California with my tennis buddy, John Carpenter. I met him in St. Louis and then we drove out... It was a beautiful cross-country trip. My new apartment was going to be in Encino California, the city where Michael Jackson grew up. Once we were within 3-4 miles of where I'd be living, I remember this car that went by us. I swear, it seemed like we were not even moving. They were going at least 120 miles per hour and then whipped off an exit. Then when we got in the apartment, as soon as I sat down, there was a good-sized earthquake and we were literally bouncing around on our seats as pictures were tilting all over the place and plates and anything else that could be jostled around was rattling. I remember saying, "Wow! What an introduction to California." My curiosity peaked and I started to wonder what was going to come at me next.

I was in Encino for only a month. I taught some tennis lessons for that month at the 3 courts that were right at the apartment. I was just getting attached to my students and had to move to Laguna Beach where my new coaching job was waiting for me. I would miss them. When I arrived at Laguna Beach, I, of course, was struck by the sheer beauty of this sleepy beach town. I've never seen more beautiful beaches, but in addition, I have never seen more beautiful girls in my life. I knew this was a whole different world awaiting me.

The first place I stayed was in a small back house, which the parents of one of the tennis players, Larry Nokes, was nice enough to set up for me. I really appreciated it and it got me my start in Laguna Beach. I had met the former women's coach, Aaron Talarico, and he was not looking forward to teaching as much Tennis. Basically, he started handing most of his clients over to me to take care of for him so he could work on his real estate. In other words, I had stepped into a gold mine.

I had a full schedule of lessons right off the bat, making $65-$75 an hour. That was really good money to me and I really felt that God had set me up for this. To me, it was a sign that I was supposed to be in Laguna Beach. How many can start a high school tennis job and have someone turn over most of their clients to you the first day you start. To say I was thankful to Aaron and to God is an understatement. I never planned to move to California and Laguna Beach. I began to tell friends that Laguna Beach chose me to live there. It had to be destiny how everything lined up so beautifully.

The first time I was on court with Aaron, he was coaching a young 14-year-old with a one-handed backhand named Benito Romeo. I asked if I could give a few tips on the backhand and Aaron was fine with it. My session with Benito went well and Benito would become my first client and I would become very close with the family. I ended up renting a room at their house for the first year I lived in Laguna. They became my west coast family.

That fall, I took over the helm of affairs as the girls' Tennis Coach for Laguna Beach high school. We had a strong team and a lot of kids on the team. There were a ton of kids on the JV team and many trying to make the varsity team, but only 14 could be in the top squad. I was giving many of those kids group and private lessons too. It was also a great way to meet parents and their kids in the Laguna Beach community. In that sense, it was a double blessing. From these connections, I met many lifelong friends.

Some of these wonderful people, including Chris Cornell, became my surfing buddies. I had both of his kids, Kendal and Cameron, on the boys and girls high school tennis team. Really good kids. Chris was the one who took me to Salt Creek Beach and told me about how surfing is not just about trying to catch a wave but enjoying nature and all the different creatures that you find in the ocean. That same day, seven dolphins swam right next to my surf board and Chris warned me not to touch them but I wanted to. They were within a foot of my surfboard. It was magical times like this that make me realize I was glad I was a risk taker and came to California. I would've never experienced this back in Michigan.

One of the parents I met from teaching the girls team was a

wonderful lady named Stephanie Berryman. She pointed out that there was a church that I might want to check out in town called little church by the sea. She was very nice and encouraging to me, so I decided to check it out. I really liked it there and there was a group of 5 pastors that would alternate preaching every week. I also found out that they had a prayer group that met at the church in a room called the upper room 6 days a week. I really liked this prayer group because the people were very passionate about seeking God and getting answers.

The leader of the upper room was Pastor Jay Grant and I really liked his straightforward approach and how passionate he was about caring about people. I really respected Pastor Jay and loved how strong his faith was. We prayed for people regularly and I saw a lot of people that were touched and even healed as I became a part of the prayer that went on there. It was a very important thing for me to find a church where I could find strength and a strong message to keep me going. Back in Michigan, I always went to church twice a week, so this was vital for me. I found some really good people at the church with strong faith who were a good association for me.

Later that fall, I heard about a tennis club called the Palisades. They had really good competition there and you could play matches every week if you had the time. It was in Newport Beach. I figured it would be a great way to meet people in the Tennis community and make some new contacts and friends. I really had a good time there, but I just wish I had spent more time there. It was pretty pricey from my vantage point, at about $200 a month but I saw it as an investment. I'm really glad I became a member. I met some of the best friends in my life from that club. I got to play the 6.0 club doubles championships and had a great partner named John Kropff, who was a young powerhouse in his early 20s. We had so many great matches in that tournament and there were hundreds of people watching, which made it exciting.

My favorite match was in the semifinals against a future friends, Daud Ahmid and Robert Vant' Hof, the former coach of the world number one, Lindsay Davenport. That match went to 9-7 in the third set and Robert even had a match point on a second serve of mine. Fortunately, Robert happened to miss that return with the backhand that barely went into the net. We ended up winning that match, but it was such a pleasure to be part of such a fantastic match I would have been happy winning or losing, especially against such classy opponents. John and I played very well in the final, squeaking out a 6-4 win in the 3rd set over John Cross and one of the teaching pros at the club, Billy McQuaid. Later in 2008 I played John Cross in another club doubles tournament but this time I lost. This time I got to feel what it was like to lose a tough match.

Me playing a two-handed backhand shot.

In my mind, I knew that losing some tough matches can be the best thing for you at times. It always got me to work harder on my game. One of my new friends from the Palisades tennis club, who I later became very close with, was a fantastic player. His name was Seth Bowen. Seth had played the same 6.0 doubles tournament that my partner and I had won and had lost in the semi-finals. When I watched him play, I could tell that his body wasn't even at 100%. They lost in the semi-finals to the team we beat in the finals. Seth was a former tour player who got up to 409 in the world, so he was at a level that I had never attained. Seth was also about 9 years older than me. He was like a big brother and in some ways, especially in the tennis realm, a mentor to me.

I remember the first time we played was at Laguna Beach high school on court number two. After playing for a while, I could tell that Seth had something in his heart he wanted to share with me. He told me some of the tough things he had been through, especially financially. Somehow, I could tell that Seth innately trusted me and felt safe sharing some of his heartfelt secrets with me. I just listened and I could tell he really needed that. This type of conversation would be a regular pattern over the years and it brought us closer as friends and brothers. The majority of these conversations happened on the tennis court, which I grew to appreciate very much. As time went on, our hits became more frequent and we began to hit at least once a week, squeezing the workouts in around my very busy work schedule.

I enjoyed teaching tennis at Laguna Beach High School. I taught many of the high school junior high and elementary kids in Laguna. This beach community environment was much different from where I grew up. Most of the kids came from a lot of money and the culture here was much more liberal than where I was from. I heard stories about the history of Laguna Beach. It was and still is known as an artist colony, but not as much as it used to be when it was cheaper to live there and there were hippies everywhere. Laguna Beach is famous also because there was the Harvard Professor turned rebel named Timothy Leary, the charismatic leader who introduced the drug, LSD, to the young hippies in that area. Soon Laguna became the central hub for the manufacturing and distribution of LSD, or Orange Sunshine, as it was called to the rest of the world. Of course, it was illegal and eventually there was a big crackdown on this operation by the police. I learned more about LSD and drug culture in Laguna Beach from a good friend and roommate named Pierce, who was many years ago right in the middle of that culture.

At one of our girls tennis matches against Sage High School, I met a very nice black gentleman named Mic Billingsly. His daughters, Rian and Devyn, were playing for Sage and they were strong players. After that day, Mic and I became friends and he hooked me up with a whole new network of junior players to coach. I met a lot of really quality people and had a lot of fun working with all these new kids. We would practice in various places, including Aliso Viejo High School. Mic was busy working, so he asked me if I could pick his girls up to go to the practices. I liked Mic and because he was such an energetic and amazing person, I was more than willing to do it.

There were many kids who filtered through this group with Billingsly's girls, but one family, besides the Mic's kids I worked with most and became good friends with was Jessica Wilcox and her parents David and Sue. We all started to go to various tournaments together along with my long-time student, Benito. We all went out to eat together and even had party gatherings together along with Mic's good friends. We had about 3 maybe 4 parties and it was a special time. At practices, Mic would at times get riled up when one of the other dads, who was a tennis coach, did some things that made Mic not trust him. He felt it wasn't fair to his girls. I tried to calm him down but that papa bear just kept coming out of him. Eventually, he chilled out later in the session.

Mic was so animated, energetic, and funny, and everything in our group seemed to center around his gigantic personality. What I admired most about Mic was how his girls were his everything. I love it when a parent loves his kids the way Mic did. I worked with Mic's kids and the ever-morphing tennis group for a little over a year. Periodically, I would get a call from Mic and he would say, "You haven't forgotten about us, have you?" I would say, "Of course, not." Then we would catch up a bit. In the fall of 2011, I heard that Mic wasn't feeling that well. Later that year, I was shocked to find out that my friend had passed. I wasn't expecting that and was totally shocked. I went to the funeral and it was so obvious that so many loved this man. Mic was a very bright positive spirit. It's so tough when you lose one of the truly good people on this planet. My journey to Southern California was just the beginning and there was much more yet to unfold.

Chapter 22

Goodbye My Friend

My first year living in Laguna Beach was quite a transition. Just the new scenery of having the luxury of being in the ocean, learning to surf, finding the right church or basically finding my tribe were all something I was in the process of doing. I remember there were times in the first year when I felt lonely like I'm not sure where I fit in and didn't feel the connection I needed with the people I knew. I was a long way from home in Michigan and I missed my friends. I met a lot of wonderful people at Little Church By The Sea and the messages were very good, but I was used to more of a Pentecostal flavor. I also knew I have a call to the inner cities of the world and felt that powerful draw pulling me to find a church that matched more of my calling. I started to go to Apostle Fred Price's church, Crenshaw Christian Center. I had seen him preach on TV and I was really impressed with his boldness, truth, and he was big on having strong faith. I thought my personality was somewhat similar to him.

As I started to go to the Crenshaw Christian Center, it did begin to feel much more like home. They also had a Tuesday service where they had really good messages and I would drive quite a long distance just to go and be a part. This was predominantly a black church, but I was very comfortable there. I had worked in the black community for 15+ years back in Michigan and I had a love for the community and a calling. I remember one time I was at one of their Tuesday Bible studies and they called people to the front for some kind of prayer and I remember I ran down there because I was excited. I remember when one of the leaders came up to me and said he could see me becoming a pastor of this church someday, which I felt was a beautiful thing to say. I just loved being there and I loved the people. I guess my enthusiasm must have touched him. I ended up going regularly to the church, twice a week and even joined. I felt I had found my new home.

One day, while at home, I decided to watch a Bishop TD Jakes' DVD. As a big Jakes' fan, I was looking forward to hearing the Bishop preach one of his eloquent powerful messages. But to my surprise, there was another tall lanky distinguished looking minister on there. His name was Bishop Noel Jones and I had heard of him before. When he started preaching, I was blown away. I don't know if I've ever heard somebody speak such powerful profound words and I knew I had to find out where he was from and if I could go see him preach live and in person. I looked him up and found out that he was in California in a town called Gardena, California, which I've never heard of. To my surprise, I found out it was under an hour away from me, not far from Crenshaw Christian Center.

So I went to my first service at Bishop Jones's church, which was called The City of Refuge. I distinctly remember sitting close to the back on the left side of the church. My hair was a little bit long at the time. I probably look like some kind of a surfer guy to them at the church. Bishop Jones' church was predominantly a black church also and I remember people looking at me like I was lost or some kind of alien. Some did not look very comfortable. I knew in time they would warm up to me if I chose to stay there. So I sat down and I locked into the message Bishop Jones was preaching and immediately he started to impact me with his message just like with the DVD. His words reached deep into my spirit and grabbed me directly by the heart. After the first message, I think I knew that, whether I wanted to admit it or not, I had found my true church home.

I had gone to the City of Refuge before I went home for Christmas and really enjoyed it. I had a great time with my family once I got home to Michigan. But then, I came back and decided to go again to what was called the Winter Revival. In that year, 2009, they had speakers that I really enjoyed, which I had seen on TV with the likes of Pastor Paula White, Bishop TD Jakes, Bishop Clarence McClendon and Pastor Sheryl Brady. When I began to go every day for the Winter Revival, which would last for two weeks, I began to like this new church more and more. I met a new friend named Carlos and he kept saying to me, "You watch. You're going to be joining here." I guess he had a feeling that I was meant to be there. I told him he didn't know what he was talking about, but in my heart I knew he was probably right.

After the Winter Revival, I kept coming to the City of Refuge. One day, Bishop Jones said something that made me realize that I was going to join the church that day. He said and I quote, "If you're in ministry, if you can't love people, until their character meets their calling, you shouldn't be in ministry." He then went on to say that people have struggles; it could be alcoholism, drug addiction, homosexuality, womanizing. He said that no matter what a person's weakness is, we need to love and pray for them till they can overcome it and step into their calling. He said that there's not one of us who doesn't have a weakness and nobody should be thrown away or judged.

When I heard him say that, I made up my mind right then and there that this is my church. I could tell that this man understood what it means to truly love people irrespective of what they're going through. He didn't judge people and that is what the love walk is all about. After service, I walked up to the front where the Bishop was and waited in line to talk to him. When I finally got to speak with him, I said, "Bishop, I was really impressed with the message, especially what you said about loving people till their character meets their calling." I told him that I could see that he truly understood the Love walk and that's what I've been looking for from a pastor. I told him I was going to join this Church because of what he said. I asked if I could ask him one more question. He agreed, so I asked, "Could you please stay alive for another thousand years?" Bishop Jones was so touched, so he said, "Don't I have your number? Well, here's mine. Call me anytime. You can call me Noel." He wrote Noel and his phone number on a paper and gave it to me.

I was shocked and very touched at the same time by his heartfelt response. He was a world famous global figure, yet so loving and down to earth. This happened way back in 2010 and since that time I can truly say that Bishop Noel Jones has been a true friend to me and has been there whenever I needed him. I rarely call him, but when I do, he always gets back to me when he gets the chance. Many times, his calls come in around two or three in the morning because he might be in Africa or some other place on the globe. But it doesn't matter; I'm just thankful that he makes time for me.

I really was looking for a pastor I could connect with and get advice from, and it really meant a lot to me that he made it so easy to approach him. I've had pastors who were disrespectful and insecure or didn't listen to me when I was sharing my ideas or my heart, and it was, at times, hurtful. Bishop Jones seems to always have the wisdom to listen respectfully, even if I may be off. He showed me he really cares. Every time I spoke with him or listened to his preaching, I felt uplifted. There was a time I felt I needed to share with Bishop my most personal business and tell him everything I was going though. I felt I could trust him and wanted to have a strong spiritual leader who could pray for me. I shared everything with him and he made it known that there is nothing you can ever tell me that will make me judge you and not love you. He was so real and genuine I was blown away.

I had a very tough season in the summer of 2012, as I almost gave up on God. It was a time I questioned God's faithfulness to me and whether He was a God that kept His word. Was He really even real... I was so upset and disgruntled that my countenance fell for the first time in my life. This downward spiraling pattern kept going on for several months. Before I knew it, I was cloaked in disappointment and bitterness. I basically looked back at my life and, as far as the major life areas, such as money, marriage and ministry were concerned, it seemed as if all the effort I put in following God was almost for nothing. I saw some results, but not even close to what I had expected after almost 25 years of serving God.

I remember talking to some ministers at the church. When they saw how negatively I was talking, they were really concerned about me and my relationship with God. I would say they were afraid for me. There was one minister, elder Jimmy Davis, who really helped me the most and stuck with me through the process. I remember I was driving home back to Laguna Beach and asked God to help me because I didn't feel like I had the strength to try anymore. I asked for wisdom, but at this point I didn't even care; I was so far gone. I realized that I had come to the edge of the abyss of giving up on God and I asked God that, although I was at the point of not caring anymore, I didn't want to be destroyed. So I asked that he protect me from myself. I remember a week or two later, as I was driving home again, God spoke to me. He said clearly to me, "Where is your faith?" It was right at this point, while driving down the 133 through the mountains of Laguna, that I had an epiphany.

God showed me my whole life span and everything that I had ever been through and I saw that there is a reason for the pain I've been through. God wanted something for me. I saw that even though I didn't have everything I wanted in the natural; that if I could praise God despite what I thought was disappointing, it meant more and had more value than having those things I wanted so badly. I had the opportunity to pass the biggest test of my life and overcome what I saw as a great disappointment and still serve God anyway. I saw that my journey had great purpose and it was a proving ground to see if God could trust me even when things were great.

Looking at it, I am astounded that God let so many years go by to see if I would stay with him, even when things didn't happen very fast. We are talking about 24, almost 25 years of waiting on God for the things I wanted most in life, which I think anyone would agree is a long time. At this point, I started to get excited cause I made a decision in my heart right then and there that I was going to start praising God because he was after something that was bigger than any millions of dollars, wife or any evangelistic position I wanted. What he wanted from me was trust no matter what. He wanted me to believe that he had my best interest at heart despite how things looked.

I remember coming to the revelation of how much I knew now that God really loved me. I remember going to church that next week and I couldn't wait to get there. I was in church with tears in my eyes, thankful that God allowed me to go through this journey for a purpose. All my journey with God had not been wasted, but it has been very vital that I went on this journey of learning to trust him. Now that I have passed this huge test, I was ready to find my niche in the church.

As I have been at The City of Refuge I have searched for where I fit there. I really enjoyed working in the altar workers prayer ministry. I loved it because I heard people's life struggles and I got to pray and encourage so many people. There's nothing like it. The leader of the alter workers is Pastor Steve Dunn who has a very gentle and loving spirit, and is very kind to all the other workers and people he interacts with. That is a big reason why I felt comfortable with this ministry.

Another ministry I got involved in after I had just gone through an awful betrayal was the music ministry. I joined the men's choir or the Men of The City (MOC for short) after a very hard time with a fellow churchgoer who had betrayed my trust. This was a very pivotal time for me. Some good friends of mine, who are now in the choir, took me in and really looked out for me when I really needed it. I was crushed at the time. My good friend, Leonard Irvine, was very helpful at that time and still a great friend till this very day.

It's amazing how a devil in your life can really hurt you, but God always has an angel waiting for you, especially if you're willing to break away from a bad situation. A big key to my recovery was making a concerted effort to genuinely forgive the person who had so deeply hurt me. I did forgive and also prayed for the person who had hurt me, as the Bible says, "Despitefully used me." That's exactly what they did, but forgiveness always makes you the winner and soon, I was flying again free from the corrupting chains of anger, revenge and hatred. "Love your enemies!!!" God kept telling me, "Love your enemies, son!!!" That kept echoing through the chambers of my heart. I embraced forgiveness and, in doing so, embraced my cross. It wasn't easy, but wisdom made it clear that I had made the right choice. It's amazing how, when I chose to walk in love and I mean love that cost me my pride, God can help you see people through his patient eyes and through a great spirit of compassion. That, to me, is such a beautiful thing. I have to say that after going through betrayal, I began to get wiser and made better friends. Some of my new friends at the time, like my great friend, Mandell Frazier, and his wife, Tonya, were a tremendous blessing to me. They are an example of people who have been givers in my life. Every time we get together, God has always been a big part of our conversations. Every time I left the fellowship, I have always gone home with my spirit uplifted, knowing I had been in the presence of people who really love me. Actually, what I love about our circle of friends, which includes several other wonderful people, is that when someone has a breakthrough in their life and, let's say it might be a tremendous financial increase, we never get jealous. Instead, we actually celebrate each other's victories. That way, everyone is a winner. I have learned to always fight to keep love for others in the air. I have changed what wealth means to me. My new kind of wealth includes being elated when my friends are reaching their dreams. This is how my close friends and I roll. We are a family.

Being in the men's choir was also like being in a family and it is a true brotherhood. We also have a tremendous men's choir leader named Patrick Bolton, who is extremely gifted at corralling all the men together and bringing the most out of our musical gifts. I really appreciate what Pat does, not to mention being a tremendous vocal talent himself. The songs he picks, plus the different suits and choir shirts we have, bring an element of style and class that makes me and the other members proud to be a part this group of men. We periodically would travel to other churches to minister and every time, the spirit would soar in those congregations. We had intertwined our hearts with theirs and all our spirits were lifted together. Those trips always brought us closer together and further deepened the purpose of our men's choir.

The last ministry, which I've been a part of only for the last 4 years is the teen ministry, ages 13-18. I came in there and really asked God to give me wisdom on how to work with these youth. Basically, I just went in and quietly served and let the kids come to me. I didn't force anything. I really was at peace there and just decided to do what I always do, which was be myself. God had over the years changed me from someone who was anxious, trying to make things happen in my own strength, to a person that trusted in him and let him open the doors himself. What I found was honestly almost miraculous.

The youth started coming to me and pulling me into their circle. Although I don't have the same skin color, we became the same spirit color and our spirits began to blend as one. Basically, we became family. In fact, Roman, who is the youth pastor's son, even nicknamed me affectionately Jamie, which was touching to me. There was one day the kids were up there praising God and dancing and having a great time and I felt God telling me to go up there and dance with them. It wasn't a big deal to me because I like to dance, but I hesitated a little bit. While I was thinking about going up, Aaron Taylor, one of the youth leaders, who I had become close to, grabbed me and we went up there and danced with them and praised God.

It was beautiful and I could see how close God was to me working with the youth. Many years before, I had dreamed and written about experiencing working in the inner city like this and now it was becoming a reality. My vision was real and God was taking me to a new place and faithfully completing what He put in my heart many years ago.

My desire to encourage people really has no geographic boundaries. I had friends that God had assigned me to where I lived in Laguna Beach also. My best friend there was my tennis buddy, Seth, who I mentioned earlier. As I mentioned earlier, our friendship started with us just playing tennis together once a week. I enjoyed the routine because our times together wasn't just about tennis; it was also life therapy. Because of the financial trial Seth was going through, including life's responsibilities, it was very important for the both of us to get our concerns and desires out of our hearts. I had my own trials, so it was great for me too. After our conversations, I always felt like my hope was growing and life was becoming more peaceful and clearer.

Many were having a rough time then. We had a lot in common because both of us had become Christians when we were in college and both of us were high-level tennis players who still played tournaments. Not only did we have good conversations in the beginning during our practices, we also had conversations during our high-level practices, where I actually was more of a student and he taught me how professional tennis players practiced. I was very fortunate to be hitting on the court with such a talented tennis player.

Eventually, after a few years went by, I began to hang out once in a while with Seth and his son, Sterling, who was only 11 or 12 years old at the time. Sterling was a gem and one of the sweetest kids you would ever meet in your life. One day, as I was walking on Oak

Street beach in Laguna Beach, I heard a loud voice. I heard this kid shouting Mr. Gleason, Mr. Gleason. I looked across the street and it was Sterling. He was so glad to see me. I felt like the most important person in the world to him. There is an indelible sweetness about him that you couldn't deny. It was very genuine. I could tell he got a lot of it from his dad. What I really liked about Seth is that he demanded honesty and that you're also timely. I liked that and our friendship grew because of that honesty. Strong friendships can only be built on trust and we were developing that slowly but surely. Seth had a nice house up in the mountains of Laguna, which was overlooking the ocean. I had fun going up there and hanging out with him and Sterling.

Seth eventually moved to a house more inland in the Laguna Audubon. He'd gotten a sweet deal. He had to give up his beautiful home in the mountains of Laguna with the ocean view and that was very hard on him. This new house was where he put up a ping-pong table in the garage and we started hanging out, having ping-pong battles between me, Sterling, and Seth. Sterling got better and better and the ping-pong battles were epic. Sterling had gotten his hand-eye coordination from his dad and he at times was kicking both our butts. We also would watch football and, of course, Seth's favorite team was Buffalo Bills because he was from Buffalo, New York. So we watched quite a few of those games too.

Seth and I began to have many strong spiritual conversations, many dealing with where God was and why our breakthrough is taking so long to happen for him and sometimes for me too. Many times, I told Seth that although he had been extremely wealthy and there was a time he lost that income, God may be humbling him and teaching him how to depend on him. I told Seth that God had humbled me too and I was learning to trust him also. I was telling Seth that maybe that's what he was trying to do with you also. We prayed together many times and I was able to share some sage wisdom with Seth, which he began to embrace and take as his own.

We both started to get into the Bible more and Seth was diligent and did devotions every morning and we would talk about that. When we went to church, it was cool because both Seth and I like to praise God. I liked to see Seth at Little Church by The Sea in Laguna

Beach where he would raise his hands and you see the biggest joyful smile come on his face. It was a smile that had joy and peace intertwined in it. Seth loved God and was chasing him.

In 2014, Seth called me one day and asked me if I would consider being his roommate. He said that the place he was living in was about to be sold and he could no longer stay there. I told him I'd think about it and get back to him after a few days. After praying, I decided I would do it. Although I loved where I was staying in Laguna Beach, I decided to move because Seth was such a valued friend. We moved in to a good-sized house in Alisa Viejo, California on January 28, 2015.

As we started to get settled there, Seth told me he was looking for a job. I told Seth to work toward becoming a tennis coach. I told him I would try to see if I could get him a job where I worked for the City of Irvine at one of the different tennis sites. I told him that he would have to get a live scan done and would have to, of course, give the City of Irvine his resume. I told him that because of the level of player he was, he should be able to get a job. Of course, I was going to put in a good word for him. I talked to my boss and he didn't think there is any reason why Seth couldn't get a job when there was a part-time position for him at one of the sites. After waiting for what seemed longer than usual, I got a call back from my boss and he said Seth didn't get the job. When I told Seth this, he was really disappointed.

He was really upset because he was counting on this job to get a fresh start in life. He applied for a few other jobs and nothing seem to be working. There were times he would be sleeping in bed and I could tell he was depressed. I told him he couldn't just sit there in bed. Sometimes, I was able to get him up and we would play tennis. He had been praying and doing his devotionals every morning diligently, but I noticed he was no longer as committed. One morning, I saw Seth drinking a beer and I said, "What the heck? Are you serious?" Then Seth said to me, "Don't you ever get tired of trying to help me." I responded, "Never, brother. I love you. I'd do anything to help you." I could tell that it really touched his heart. A couple of days later, in the morning, Seth said he wanted to show me something. He pointed to his eyes and went into the bathroom where there's better light. He said, "Look at my eyes; there's a dimness to them. There's no light in them anymore." When I looked, I noticed it too. The regular spark that was in his eyes wasn't there anymore. I was a bit shocked as was he... After that day, I tried to think of things that'd up lift Seth's spirit. I was starting a Men's Success group along with a few other men from church. I invited Seth to come join us. I remember I had my friend, Matt, on the phone and we were both excited about the upcoming meeting. When I asked if he wanted to come too, he said it wasn't the right time for him.

Then one morning, in April, I sent a text to Seth, which said, "Good morning, my brother in Christ. God bless you. I hope you're having a great day." I was at the beach at the time and Seth texted me back and asked if I was coming back to the house or going about my day. I told him I'd be back there in about 45 minutes. I came back an hour and a half later. When I opened the door and looked inside, I saw it, but it didn't look real. It was as if time stood still. Seth had hung himself from a rope. When I first saw it, I was hoping it was a joke, but it wasn't. Everything was so quiet. When I collected myself and realized what was going on, I ran over and got scissors to cut him down to hopefully save his life. I had to cut him down myself and he fell into my arms and I laid him on the ground very gently. I was in total shock. I was too late; I could not save him. After trying to revive him, I had one unforgettable thought come to my mind and that was: this is what it would have been like taking Jesus down from the cross. For whatever reason, that came to my mind at that moment very vividly. The first person I called was Pastor Jay Grant and he said that I should call 911 immediately.

I was not there by myself for long. The cops came and asked me questions and there were grief counselors sent to talk to me. I was there for 3 hours or so and had to tell Jen (Sterling's mom) and she, in turn, had to tell Seth's son, Sterling. For whatever reason, I had the strength to take in and deal with the tragic loss of my best friend. Again, I felt the echoes of my past looking at me and choosing me. Just like when I witnessed my mom break down when I was 3 years old, tragedy had chosen me again. I thought that to protect Sterling, I would have to take what tragedy had to offer that day. Looking back, I see clearly that God's grace was sufficient that day.

Somehow, I was calm in the storm, but maybe I was in shock and just numb from all of it. I talked to two Pastors from the City of Refuge -- Pastor Seth Gaiters and Pastor Hosea Collins. Pastor Hosea strongly recommended that I should not be alone. He advised that I even come to Wednesday service that same day so that I could have support and be prayed for. When I shared what had happened, everyone stopped what they were doing and focused their energy and prayers on me and my wellbeing. I felt the love and the strength of their prayers and they were lifting me with a strength I didn't possess at the time. They prayed for me and they, especially, prayed to protect my mind from the image I saw that day. I'll never forget what those beautiful people did for me that day in my time of need. That ended up being a very important prayer for me. After that prayer at my church, I had to find some close friends to stay with that night.

I had to get out of that house immediately to survive this... My good friend, Garry Glaub, a tennis coach in Laguna let me sleep on an air mattress at his place for 3 weeks and his studio was not a big place. His dog, Whitney, a very sweet black lab was good for me to be around. We, of course, talked about what happened but also watched TV together. We were just friends. I needed friends to occupy my thoughts all the time. We both shared our anger that Seth chose to leave us, almost as if we had been cheated of the things we could go experience with him in the future. That thought was one of the hardest pills I had to swallow. I was never going to get to do the fun things and dreams we had talked about with my great friend. That was taken away from me and many others forever. After staying at Garry's, I stayed for 3 months at the Romeo's house and slept on the couch and eventually on my air mattress.

They literally were like my second family, even before this tragedy, so I could not have been at a better place. Vittorio, the dad and Benito and Dino, his sons, were beautiful for me to be around. Sara, Vito's daughter, wasn't around as much at that time. Another friend of mine, John Schaarsmith, who I eventually called, Johnny Boy during my stay there, was very good to me also. John was one of the tenants at the Romeo household. We had fun and watched tons of movies, especially Netflix shows, which became addictive to me. I had never done that before, and having my thoughts occupied during this time with fun, friends or work was the best thing for me.

Yes, I was escaping. Even though I was escaping many times, I would walk around and just start sobbing. I had a heaviness in me that wouldn't go away. I missed my friend, my brother, Seth. I missed his voice - that booming voice - and that hearty laugh that you could hear from a mile away. Seth had love for not only me but everyone who had the opportunity to get to know him. He was gentle and loving to us all. I couldn't talk to him anymore and I couldn't believe this was real. I realized that there was a scar on my heart and that it was permanent. Seth would always be with me, but he took some of me with him to heaven. I knew I would never be the same.

Not long after Seth passed, God gave me three visions of Seth and all three let me know that he was with God. I needed to know this and it put my heart to rest. The third vision I will tell you about. I had just called my tennis buddy, Ginger, who was also a very close friend of Seth. I was just walking down the stairs to Oak Street beach when I was led to call Ginger. Of course, we started to talk about Seth as I slowly walked down the steps to Oak street beach. After talking for about 10 minutes, I stopped mid-sentence and said, "Ginger!!! I see Seth. He's on the beach with me." I knew at that moment I was in a totally different dimension because in my mind I could clearly see Seth about 50 yards down the beach looking right at me, kind of gazing at me with a calm look, like he was looking for me.

I kept looking at him and he looked so relaxed and happy. As I continued to look, he would peer out at the ocean just gazing into the distance and I could tell a breeze was blowing against him. I, at that moment, remembered how he said before he passed that he never wanted to move away from the ocean. The happiness I saw in him at that moment gave this encounter extra meaning. I was so happy to see Seth free from any pain. I began to walk very slowly down the beach and I was giving Ginger the play-by-play, as I was watching Seth. It seemed like every step I took Seth would take a step also towards me and little by little he kept getting closer to me. This went on for about 45 minutes. And before I knew it, Seth was right next to me and just walking with me with a very gentle smile on his face. I felt that he was just making sure I was alright. I told Seth something deep from my heart and that I really needed to see him again. I said I really missed him. As we kept walking, we finally came to a stop on the beach. Together, we both gazed out at the ocean and then he put his hand on my shoulder and told me something I'll never forget. He said, "I love you, Jimmy, and I came to thank you for being there for me." We just sat there together looking at the ocean for a few more moments together and I sensed it was time for him to go. I didn't fight it; I just let it happen and watched Seth walk away. I saw him look back at me with a gentle smile and a nod. As I watched him go, after a short while, he disappeared. Ginger was so excited to hear that I had encountered Seth again and I realized God had given me something precious and that was a final communion with my best friend, Seth, before he passed into eternity.

Within a couple of weeks, after Seth's passing, I went to the Canyon courts in Laguna Beach to talk to the tennis community. They all knew and loved Seth very much. When I walked through the door to the courts, many of Seth's friends were there and everybody just stopped what they were doing and froze and looked at me. I just slowly walked toward them, looking at all of them on the brink of tears. Soon, we all embraced in one big cluster and just held each other, all of us wishing that our brother, Seth, was still with us. We talked and it was the 1st time I got really emotional and completely lost it. All these beautiful people—Peter Nez, Ray, Glenn Parrish, and Ginger Dahlem—were there for me and I was there for them. We all had a cry together. Everyone's heart was torn and aching. This was a major loss to our tennis community in Laguna because Seth was loved by pretty much everybody. We all needed each other to get through this. I don't think Seth had enemies. He was too genuine and giving to everyone. Together, we were all going to get through this. Somehow, we would do it.

Something happened at this time, which made this experience extremely hard for me. It was something I didn't have the strength to handle at the time. My landlord at the house Seth and I rented in Aliso Viejo would not let me get out of the lease. He said I still had to pay rent for the 8 remaining months of my contract. I knew I couldn't stay there and survive it. My heart was already broken into 1 million pieces from losing Seth and now I had to deal with the anger I had towards my landlord, Mr. Wong, who I thought was being so inconsiderate and insensitive to what I was going through.

I was extremely angry with him. After three months of being away from that house, there came the day I actually had to move back in mid-August of that year. By that time, I had changed my heart toward Mr. Wong. I had been going through this awful dialog full of manipulation and threats from Mr. Wong, and Kent Bowen was helping me navigate all of this the 3 months I had been going through it. Thank God for Kent and the Bowen family who were looking out for me. One day, as I was on the phone as usual with Kent building up a good mad about my landlord, I suddenly felt a shift in my heart. I said to Kent, "We aren't handling this right and it's important that no matter what happens we need to pray for Mr. Wong and forgive him. That's what God would want us to do."

As soon as I said that, I knew it was the right thing to do and I felt a release in my heart and automatically started feeling more peace. Kent paused on the phone and then said, "You are right, brother. You're absolutely spot on." I knew God was challenging us to forgive Mr. Wong despite what I was going through. Thank God for Kent, he was always there for me through the whole 3-month ordeal. And because of him, we never end our conversations without a strong prayer. Prior to that moment, I used to call the house a tomb because of what had happened there. After forgiving Mr. Wong, I changed the house's name to a house of praise. I prayed that God was going to do a miracle in my life and I would be healed from all of this pain. God was all I had and I put my faith in him. I knew in my heart that forgiving Mr. Wong was a test of forgiveness and somehow I found it in my heart to forgive this man who had made my life so hard. True healing began only after I chose to forgive Mr. Wong, and I knew that was the truth.

I remember I had to stay at the house in Aliso Viejo all by myself the first night. I was scared and I facebooked people to pray for me. I put the air mattress right by the door in case I wanted to run out of the house at any time. Somehow, I got through that first night. I could not believe I was actually staying there. I had faith that God was there with me though I knew I could do it. As time went by, I got used to being back at the house, but I never really liked it; I just accepted it and believed there was a reason I was going through this. I still tried not to be there, though.

Months passed by and before I knew it, December was on the horizon. I was really looking forward to going on my annual trip home to Michigan for Christmas to see my family and friends. I, especially, needed family at this time. God continued to send angels of encouragement up until my flight home. The Bible says, "There is healing in His wings." As the jet took off, I thought of that scripture immediately as I looked at one of the mighty wings of that jet. Somehow, I knew I was going to be alright. Yes, I was going to be alright.

Wisdom Nugget

40) Forgive & Obey. PASS THE TEST: I was shattered and going through so much hell after Seth died and couldn't get out of my lease. Somehow, even though I was very angry and hurt, I prayed for wisdom and felt led to forgive my landlord. I'm glad I forgave him because anger was beginning to consume me. God gave me the choice to hate or forgive. I believe God's love impressed me to have compassion on my landlord, which gave me the power to forgive him. I sensed that things were about to get very bad for me if I didn't obey God. I decided to pass the forgiveness test. It wasn't easy, but I'm thankful I made the right choice.

www.ingramcontent.com/pod-product-compliance
Lightning Source LLC
Chambersburg PA
CBHW070618300426
44113CB00010B/1573